No. 616

Rev. W. Henry Brooks,
from his Father.
Oct. 1, 1867.

TERRA MARIÆ;

OR

THREADS OF MARYLAND COLONIAL HISTORY.

BY

EDWARD D. NEILL,

ONE OF THE SECRETARIES OF THE PRESIDENT OF THE UNITED STATES.

Nec falsa dicere, nec vera reticere.

PHILADELPHIA:

J. B. LIPPINCOTT & CO.

1867.

TO

GEORGE PEABODY,

A native of the Massachusetts Colony;

Preferring the title of American Citizen, and

Friend of the London Poor,

To Heraldic Honors from a noble Queen;

Known as the princely patron of Literature in his native land, especially in the

CITY OF BALTIMORE,

Where he passed many years of early manhood;

and as a patriot above sectional prejudice;

THIS LITTLE WORK

Is inscribed by a stranger,

Whose paternal ancestors dwelt in the

Colony of Maryland.

PREFACE.

OLDMIXON, when he wrote the history of the British Colonies in America, more than a hundred and fifty years ago, complained that he had failed to obtain the information sought, relative to the Maryland Colony.

Chalmers, a Scotch lawyer in Baltimore City, returning to England after the revolutionary struggle began, in his general colonial history, commenced at the suggestion of Sir John Dalrymple, supplied to some extent the deficiency. Bozman, in the present century, has done valuable service in bringing to light old records, but in condemning the bigotry of an intolerant age, himself, as is too often the case, becomes uncharitable. McMahon, an able jurist, has presented, in clear, concise language, a valuable historical view of the Government of Maryland, and the only regret, after reading it, is that the author did not publish another volume, as was contemplated. McSherry, the last of the historians of the State, adds much concerning the revolutionary period and the present century, but views subjects too much from a denominational stand-point.

When not employed in official duties at the Executive Mansion, it has been a recreation to visit the Capitol, and pushing by the jostling throng, constantly shuffling over the marble tiles of the rotunda, to hasten into the quiet alcoves of the noble library of Congress, there to rummage the folios of Strafford, Winwood, Kennett, Rushworth, Thurloe, and Journals of the House of Lords and Commons, the quarto volumes of Fuller, Anthony Wood, and Hazard, also not the less valuable because smaller, the Calendar of British State Papers, the publications of the Camden Society, the Somers and Force Historical Tracts, and numerous other valuable works of reference. As the result of this turning over of pages, numberless as the leaves of autumn, I have picked out a few threads of the colonial history of Maryland which I had never seen before, and as they were interesting to me, I have thought they might please the public. It affords me pleasure to take this opportunity, to acknowledge the courtesy I have received from the librarian and his assistants in my investigations.

E. D. N.

Anacostan Ridge,
near Washington, D. C ,
February 1, 1867.

CONTENTS.

TERRA MARIÆ.

CHAPTER I.

THE FIRST LORD BALTIMORE.

YORKSHIRE, three centuries ago, was a remote county, in the north of England, and under favorable circumstances, a six days' journey from London was necessary to reach its wooded mountain slopes and barren moors. While the Cathedral of York was then, as now, justly admired for its lofty tower, and as the largest and finest in the whole kingdom, the hamlets were few; Leeds numbered four or five thousand poor fullers and weavers, and Sheffield was "a singularly miserable place, containing about two thousand inhabitants, of whom a third were half-starved and half-naked beggars."[1]

[1] Macaulay.

The yeomanry, however, though rude and coarse, were brave and honest, and a few ancient families scattered among them, were equal in talents and culture with any in the country, among whom were the Fairfaxes,[1] Wentworths,[2] and Calverts, all of whom have remote descendants in the United States of America.

George Calvert, the first Lord Baltimore, was

---

[1] William Fairfax, for a time Governor of the Bahamas, afterward held office under the Crown in New England, and here he married his second wife at Salem, Massachusetts. Invited by his relative, Lord Fairfax, to take charge of his estates, he moved to the vicinity of Mount Vernon. He had two sons, of whom the younger, the Rev. Bryan Fairfax, became the eighth Lord Fairfax. The present representative, Charles, lives in California, and his brother, Dr. John Fairfax, in Maryland, a few miles from Washington. Washington, in a letter to the Earl of Buchan, April 20th, 1793, says:

"The family of Fairfax, of which you speak, is also related to me. * * * * What remains of the old stock are near neighbors to my estate of Mount Vernon. The late Lord Thomas Fairfax, with whom I was perfectly acquainted, at a distance of sixty miles from me, after he had removed from Belvoir, the seat of his kinsman, which adjoins my estate just mentioned, and is going to be inhabited by a younger member of the family as soon as the house, which was some years ago burnt down, can be rebuilt."

[2] William Wentworth, a member of this old Yorkshire family, emigrated to New Hampshire about the time that Leonard Calvert came to Maryland. His descendants were John, Benning, Sir John, all Colonial Governors, John, a member of the Continental Congress: and John, member of the Thirty-ninth Congress from Chicago, Illinois, is also of the same family.

the son of Leonard Calvert[1] and his wife, Alice Croxall, and was born at Kipling.

When only eleven years of age, in 1593, he entered Trinity College, Oxford, and in four years became a Bachelor of Arts. As a student he displayed a fondness for literature, and before he graduated, a poem from his pen, an elegy upon the death of Henry Unton,[2] English Ambassador at the Court of France, was published.

As was customary after leaving college, he made a tour to the Continent, and upon his return married, and became the clerk of Sir Robert Cecil, Earl of Salisbury. In this way he was brought into the presence, and attracted the attention of, the half-crazed, half-pedant monarch, King James. In 1605, on the occasion of the King visiting the University of Oxford, he received the degree of Master of Arts.

He was frequently sent abroad on public business, and having returned from Paris, he wrote on March the tenth, 1610, the following chatty

---

1 Leonard Calvert, of Yorkshire, the father of Lord Baltimore, although not one of the nobility of England, appears to have been a very respectable person. Eleanor Calvert, of Mount Airy, Maryland, the granddaughter of Benedict Calvert, was married to John Parke Custis, the son of Mrs. George Washington by a former husband. The Hon. Charles Calvert, of the Thirty-seventh Congress, lately deceased at Riversdale, Maryland, near Washington, was also a descendant. All of the American family have a baton in their coat of arms

2 Unton, a brave and much-esteemed Ambassador.

letter to Sir Thomas Edmondes, then resident as Ambassador:

"But that I could not let pass any servant of your own, without saluting you, I should perhaps have stayed a few days longer for more matter; desiring, together with the advertisement of my safe arrival, to let your Lordship understand the state of our Court here, our country, and our friends.

"But I am yet but a stranger, and know little, and besides, the extraordinary good usage I received from your Lordship and your worthy Lady, which I preach to all my friends here; with that acknowledgment which it deserveth, hath so debauched me, as my spirits are still with you, and I cannot yet well draw them from the Faubourg of St. Germain, to intend anything here.

"I arrived in England, at Hythe, in Kent, upon Saturday last, late at night, having been six days and one night at sea, with foul weather, and upon Sunday I came hither, where I was not unwelcome nor unlooked for, as I perceived. I presently went to the Court and delivered your dispatch. I found my Lord in a disposition calm and sweet, using me with that favorable respect wherewith he is pleased to grace those poor servants he makes account of.

"He read not your letter presently, being at that time in hand, as it seemed, with some other dispatch; neither had I any other speech with him, of your Lordship, than that he asked me, how you did?; when I remembered your service to him. He dismissed me for that night because it was very late, and since I have seen him but once; for the next day he went to Hatfield, and from thence is gone to the King at Royston, and to Audley End, where my Lord Chamberlain is at this present, and returns again hither within these three days, as I understand. * * * *

"I had forgotten to put with the news of the Clergy, a famous conversion of a revolted minister of our Church, Mr. Theophilus Higgins,[1] who, your Lordship may remember, fled from England to Brussels some three or four years since, and was undertaken by Sir Edward Hoby, who wrote an 'Anti-Higgins,' answered afterwards, as I take it, in part or in whole by my Lady Lovell.

---

[1] Theophilus Higgins, at the age of fourteen, in 1592, went to Oxford, and received an A.M. in 1600. Was a good Latin poet. Preached at St. Dunstan's, London, and was very popular. Under Jesuit influence, joined the Church of Rome, and spent two years at Douay. He published his reasons for the change in 1609, in a pamphlet called his "First Motive to Adhere to the Roman Church."

The sermon alluded to in Calvert's letter was published with this title:

"Sermon at St. Paul Cross, March 3d, 1610, on Eph. ii. 4, 5, 6, 7, In Testimony of his hearty Reunion with the Church of England, and his hearty Submission thereto. London, 1611."

2

"This Mr. Higgins, upon Sunday last, the day of my arrival, preached, at Paul's Cross, his penitential sermon, when were present my Lord Treasurer, and divers other Lords of the Council, besides an infinite number of all sorts of people. The self-same day was born to Sir Edward Hoby[1] a son and heir, inasmuch as he saith he will bless that day for the birth of two children, a spiritual and temporal; for a *natural* I dare not say, though perhaps more proper for this division, because this word sometimes receives a base interpretation.

"And yet himself said, as I hear, as soon as the midwife brought him his son to see him, that 'it was a goodly child, God bless him! and wonderfully like his father, whosoever he were.'"

In a few months Calvert was made the Clerk of the Privy Council, and soon became a favorite attendant of James the First, and accompanied him to Royston. "In his journey," saith one, "Calvert, Clerk of the Council, is settled about him, and is wholly employed in reading and writing."

During this journey of 1611 James commenced the tractate anathematizing Vorstius, the succes-

---

[1] Hoby was educated at Oxford, and knighted in 1582. He was a well-read man. The title of the pamphlet alluded to as "Anti-Higgins," was: "A Letter to Mr. Theophilus Hygons, late Minister, now a Fugitive, in answer to his First Motive." He died in 1616.

sor of Arminius in the University of Leyden, which was written out and completed by Calvert. In consequence of his acquaintance with foreign languages, he was also at this time intrusted with the Italian and Spanish correspondence, a position under the Commonwealth occupied by John Milton.

Another correspondent writes to a friend abroad under date of February the twentieth, 1618–19:

"The King went to Theobalds on Tuesday, but before his going, Sir George Calvert was sworn Secretary. I had an inkling of it two or three days before, though the patent was drawn with a blank, and the voice ran generally with Packer. The night before he was sworn, the Lord of Buckingham[1] told him the King's resolution, but he disabled himself divers ways, but specially, that he thought himself unworthy to sit in that place, so lately possessed by his noble lord and master. The King was well pleased

---

[1] George Villiers, Duke of Buckingham, and his mother, exercised great influence over James the First. He was distinguished for his personal symmetry, as his master was for his clumsiness. An old writer said: "As Ammianus describes a well-shaped man, ab ipso capite usque ad unguium summitates recta erat lineamentorum compage; from the nails of his fingers, nay, from the sole of his foot to the crown of his head, there was no blemish in him. And yet his carriage and every stoop of his deportment, more than his excellent form, were the beauty of his beauty." He was assassinated by Felton in 1628.

with his answer and modesty; and sending for him, asked many questions, most about his wife. His answer was, that she was a good woman, and had brought him ten children; and would assure his Majesty that she was not a wife with a witness. This, and some other passages of this kind, seem to show that the King is in a great vein for taking down high-handed women."

With increasing influence, in 1617 he was knighted, and now appears in the public records as Sir George Calvert.

Under the malign influence of Gondomar, the Spanish Ambassador, the King ordered the arrest of Sir Walter Raleigh, in July, 1618, and disgraced England by beheading him three months afterward in the old Palace-yard. It is with pain that we read of Calvert's intimacy with the Spaniard, of his visits to the gallant navigator in prison, and of his calling at his house and taking therefrom his sea-charts, a manuscript on the art of war, and another containing an account of all the sea-ports in the world.

While King James tried to satisfy the English people by assenting to laws for the suppression of Popery, he manifested no antipathy to any of his friends with inclinations in that direction, and in February complimented Calvert by making him Secretary of State for life. To the plea of inability to perform the duties of the office, Buckingham said it was the King's own choice, and in a day or two the oath of office was administered, and a letter written on April the nineteenth, says: "Secretary Calvert keeps about the King, and has most of the employment."

In the year 1613 he was appointed one of the Commissioners to go to Ireland to examine the condition of affairs, and to listen to grievances.

It was rumored about this time that he would be appointed Ambassador to the States General, and a friend of Sir Dudley Carleton, the incumbent, wrote: "I have both before and since made all the inquiry I could, and can find no ground of any fresh report. Only I have heard Mr. Calvert named, but when the question is asked him he doth utterly renounce any such intention in himself, and I do rather believe him, for that it is not likely he should affect such a journey, being reasonably well settled at home, and having a wife and many children, which are no easy carriage, specially so far."

The whimsical monarch not only conferred honors, but rewards. The next year he received a grant of the increased custom on silk for twenty-one years, and an annual pension or one thousand pounds.

The reckless expenditure of James, and his constant grant of monopolies, had created great dissatisfaction among the masses, and it was desirable that he should have as many friends as possible in the Parliament of 1621, and for this reason Calvert, with Wentworth, offered himself as a member from Yorkshire.

Their opponent was Sir John Saville, a man of considerable influence; and it is interesting to read the electioneering correspondence of the impetuous Wentworth previous to the day of election.

With an energy and rapidity not excelled by the most successful politician of the nineteenth century, he wrote several letters daily during the campaign, and was profuse in promises and delicate flattery. The following extracts from letters of the same period, attest the energy of the man. To Sir Thomas Fairfax he writes:

"I was at London much entreated, and, indeed, at last enjoined, to stand with Mr. Secretary Calvert for to be knight of this shire the next Parliament, both by my Lord Clifford and himself; which, after I had assented unto and dispatched my letters, I perceived that some of your friends had motioned the like to Mr. Secretary on your behalf, and were therein engaged, which was the cause I write no sooner unto you. Yet, hearing by my cousin Middleton that he, moving you in my behalf for your voices, you were not only pleased to give over that intendment, but freely to promise us your best assistance, I must confess that I cannot forbear any longer to write unto you how much this courtesy deserves of me;

and that I cannot chose but take it most kindly from you as suitable with the ancient affection which you have always borne me and my house.

"And presuming of the continuance of your good respects toward me, I must entreat the company of yourself and friends with me at dinner on Christmas-day, being the day of the election, when I shall be most glad of you, and then give you further thanks for your kind respects."

To one he writes: "In my next letters I will let Mr. Secretary know your good respect and kindness toward him, whereof I dare assure you he will not be unmindful."

To another he says: "I have got an absolute promise that if I be chosen knight that you shall have a burgess-ship (reserved for me) at Appleby, wherewith I must confess I am not a little pleased, in regard we shall sit there, judge, and laugh together."

To a relative he makes a suggestion: "The course my Lord Darcy and I hold is, to entreat the high-constables to desire the petty constables to set down the names of all freeholders within their townships, and which of them have promised to be at York and bestow their voices with us, so as we may keep the note as a testimony of their good affections, and know whom we are beholden unto; desiring them further to go along with us to York, on Sunday, being Christmas-eve, or else meet us about two o'clock of the day at Tadcaster. I desire you would please to deal effectually with your high-constables, and hold the same course, that so we may be able to judge what number we may expect out of your wapentake. I hope you will take the pains to go along with us, together with your friends, to York, that so we may all come in together, and take part of an ill dinner with me the next day, when yourself and friends shall be right heartily welcome."

Sir Arthur Ingram is informed: "As touching the election we now grow to some heat; Sir John Saville's instruments closely and cunningly suggesting underhand, Mr. Secretary's non-residence, his being the King's servant, and out of these reasons by law cannot, and, in good discretion, ought not, be chosen of the country.

"Whereas himself is their martyr, having suffered for them; the patron of the clothiers; the fittest to be relied on, and that he intends to be at York on the day of election."

To Calvert he gives a history of the condition of things and the state of feeling in the County: "May it please you, sir, the Parliament writ is delivered to the sheriff, and he, by his faithful promise, deeply engaged for you. I find the gentlemen of these parts generally ready to do you service. Sir Thomas Fairfax stirs not; but Sir John Saville, by his instruments, exceeding busy, intimating to the common sort underhand, that yourself being not resident in the County, cannot by law be chosen, and being his Majesty's Secretary and a stranger, one not safe to be trusted by the country; but all this, according to his manner, so closely and cunningly as if he had no part therein; neither doth he, as yet, further declare himself, than only, that he will be at York the day of the election; and thus finding he cannot work them from me, labors only to supplant you. My Lord President hath writ to his freeholders on your behalf, and seeing he will be in town on the election-day, it were, I think, very good if he would be pleased to show himself for you in the Castle-yard, and that you writ a few lines unto him, taking notice that you hear of some opposition, and therefore desire his presence. I have heard that when Sir Francis Darcy opposed Sir Thomas Lake in a matter of like nature, the *Lords of the Council writ to Sir Francis to desist.* I know my Lord Chancellor is very sensible of you in this business, *a word to him and such a letter would make an end of all.*"

The Christmas of 1620, in old York, was a day long remembered. To the usual hilarities of the season were added the crowd and confusion of an exciting election. Amid the drinking of tankards of ale and cups of gooseberry wine, there was angry discussion of the merits of the contestants, emphasized with round and coarse

Saxon oaths, until toward night the cheers for Wentworth and Calvert decided the contest.

Previous to the assembling of Parliament public opinion was decidedly against James. An intelligent foreigner wrote: "Consider for pity's sake what must be the state and condition of a prince, whom the preachers publicly from the pulpit assail; whom the comedians of the metropolis covertly bring upon the stage; whose wife attends these representations in order to enjoy the laugh against her husband; whom the Parliament braves and despises, and who is universally hated by the whole people."

One could not walk the streets of London, without hearing denunciatory language, nor enter the bookstores without beholding on the counters ludicrous caricatures, and sarcastic pamphlets aimed at the King. In the library of the antiquary, Sir Robert Cotton, were frequently closeted Pym, Selden, Coke, and other brave and talented men, to arrange plans of opposition against the monarch who had announced that "he would govern according to the good of the Commonwealth, but not according to the common will."

At the opening of the Parliament, James, in his address, said: "It is the King that makes laws, and ye are to advise him to make such as will be best for the Commonwealth."

Calvert stood firm for the royal prerogatives as thus interpreted, and early in the session urged Parliament to accede to the demands for money, and to say less about their liberties and freedom of speech; and his course was so decided, that he "was censured for his forwardness."[1]

Wentworth, his colleague, had still sympathies with the people, and was perplexed by the state of affairs. In a letter to his brother-in-law, Lord Clifford, he wrote: "The path we are like to walk in is now more narrow and slippery, yet not so difficult but may be passed with circumspection, patience, and principally, silence."

The discussions of Parliament, involving as they did the principles of the British Constitution, the alleged bribery of so great a man as Lord Bacon, and the proposed marriage of Prince Charles to the Infanta of Spain, are still perused by the lover of civil and religious liberty with deep interest.

---

[1] "The first day of their sitting, Secretary Calvert made a speech for supply of the King's wants, which was thought untimely, before anything else was treated of. * * * There was some crossing and contestation 'twixt Secretary Calvert and Coke at a Committee about the Spanish Ambassador, who is said to have almost as many come to his mass, as to the sermon at St. Andrew's over against him, and there is great complaint of the increase of Popery everywhere."—*Chamberlain to Carleton, Feb.* 10*th*, 1620–21.

"The next day they met, which I think was on Monday, Secretary Calvert begins to speak, that his Majesty thought the first motion for obtaining liberty of speaking was very unreasonable."—*Mead to Stuteville, Feb.* 10*th*, 1620–21.

When in November they were preparing a petition to the King, asking that the Prince might form a Protestant alliance, Calvert mentioned these proceedings to King James, which so enraged him that he instantly sent a letter to the Speaker, complaining of the "fiery, popular, and turbulent spirits" in the lower House, and forbidding them to inquire into the mysteries of State, or to concern themselves about the marriage of his son. The letter was arrogant and menacing, and roused Pym and others to protest, which terrified the Court: and Calvert, trying to still the storm, admitted the closing expressions of the King's to be incapable of defense, "calling them a slip of the pen at the close of a long answer." The apology was of no avail, and the Commons firmly asserted that there should be freedom of debate, and "from all impeachment, imprisonment, and molestation," for anything said in the discussions of Parliament: and the King, coming to London, declared the protestation to be null, and tore it out of the records, dissolved the Parliament, and imprisoned Coke, Pym, Selden, and others.

After this he granted indulgence to the Roman Catholics, and an order was sent to the judges, "that in their several circuits they discharge all prisoners for church recusancy, or for refusing the oath of supremacy, or for dispersing Papist books, or for hearing or saying mass."

Shortly after the close of Parliament, Wentworth moved to his country seat in Yorkshire, where both himself and wife were sick from fever contracted in London, and the latter, the eldest daughter of the Earl of Cumberland, died.

During the same summer, Calvert was attached to his friend, by another and more powerful tie, a common affliction, which is thus announced in a letter written on August the tenth, 1622, and by a correspondent of Sir Dudley Carleton: "Two days since Secretary Calvert's lady went away in childbirth, leaving many little ones behind her."

Not long after this sorrow, Sir George Calvert's eldest son married Anna, daughter of Thomas Earl Arundel, one of the most influential Roman Catholic noblemen in the realm. For months, he was now busily employed as principal Secretary of State, in preparing the articles for the intended marriage of Charles with the Infanta of Spain, which were, when completed, sworn to by the King in the presence of the two Spanish Ambassadors and twenty-four privy councillors.

Calvert had most devoutly wished for the consummation of this marriage, and it was with great pleasure that he read a letter on February the twenty-seventh, 1623, by an associate secretary, informing him that the Prince and the Duke of Buckingham, ten days before, disguised, and with the assumed names of Jack and Tom Smith, had quietly sailed for Madrid.

To prevent excitement in England, all communications from the party in Spain were first transmitted in cypher to him, and then written out and read to the anxious King. A letter from the Secretary to Buckingham has been preserved, which we give in full:

MAY IT PLEASE YOUR LORDSHIP—

All I have to say now is humbly to thank you for your last favor, in remembering me with a letter, though it is more than I look for. It shall be enough at all times, if it please your Lordship, that I may understand your commandments by Mr. Francis Cottington, and that I remain in your favor. Here is amongst all men an universal joy for the good news brought us by Mr. Grymes,[1] and we have made the best expressions of it we can for the present.

I hope it shall every day increase; first, for the general good, and next, for the great part of honor your Lordship hath in it, wherein God make you as happy as ever man was! And so I rest,

Your Lordship's humble
And most faithful servant,
GEO. CALVERT.

St. Martin's Lane, 3 April, 1623.

---

[1] Grymes, gentleman of the horse to Buckingham.

In the year 1624 both Wentworth and Calvert were members of Parliament, the latter now representing Oxford. Owing to sickness, Wentworth was detained for a brief period at his country seat, and on recovery wrote, on April the twenty-eighth, to his former colleague:

"Matter worthy your trouble these parts afford none, where our objects and thoughts are limited in looking upon a tulip, hearing a bird sing, a rivulet murmuring, or some such petty yet innocent pastime, which for my part I begin to feed myself in, having, I praise God, recovered more in a day, by an open country air, than in a fortnight's time in that smothering one of London. By my troth, I wish you divested of the importunity of business, here for a half dozen hours; you should taste how free and fresh we breathe, and how, procul metu fruimur modestis opibus, a wanting sometimes, to persons of greater eminency in the administration of commonwealths."

Although deeply interested in home affairs, Calvert had, like the rest of the public men of his age, endeavored to obtain wealth by colonizing the New World.

He was not only a member of the Virginia Company, but on July the fifth, 1622, he and Daniel Gookin Gent were voted by the New England Company to be admitted as members of the association, and about this time he received a grant for the whole country of Newfoundland, which was recalled, and on March the thirtieth, 1623, a new grant issued, with alteration and addition of some particular points for better encouraging that plantation, which was again modified on the seventh of April, and letters patent issued to Sir George Calvert, his heirs and assigns, forever, of all that entire portion of land situate within Newfoundland, and all islands within ten leagues of the eastern shore thereof, to be incorporated into a province called Avalon.[1]

The affairs of the Virginia Company were at this time in great confusion, factions prevailed in the colony, and among the Directors at home. The Earl of Southampton, Lord Cavendish, Sir Ed. Sackville, and Sir Edwin Sandys, the leaders of one side, and the Earl of Warwick and others, the leaders of the opposition. A few days after the Newfoundland patent was issued, they appeared before the King with their grievances, and Sackville bore himself so insolently that the King "was fain to take him down soundly and roundly," and on the fourteenth of May Calvert

---

[1] Lord Baltimore's colony was begun in 1620. Whitbourne, in his description of Newfoundland, published in 1622, says: "The Right Hon. Sir George Calvert, Secretary to the King's most excellent Majesty, hath undertaken to plant a colony of his Majesty's subjects in the country, and hath already most worthily sent thither in these last two years a great number, with all means for their livelihood, and they are building houses, clearing off land, and making salt."

wrote, under instructions, that the election of officers, which the King recommended to the especial care of the Virginia Company, was yesterday, by the King, in council, ordered to be put off.

The dissatisfaction with the company arose out of the greed, that had been manifested to enrich themselves to the discomfort of the settlers in the plantations, and also because of the "popularness of the government," the legislative assembly in Virginia being decidedly democratic in its views.

The colony was really in a forlorn condition, and after fifteen years of care numbered only twelve hundred and seventy-five whites, seventy-six of whom lived on the Eastern Shore, and twenty-two negroes.

The General Assembly of Virginia, in a statement of their grievances under Sir Thomas Smythe's government, draw a picture which seems too frightful to be literally received. "The allowances of food in those times," said they, "for a man was loathsome, and not fit for beasts; many fled for relief to the savages, but were taken again, and hung, shot, or broken on the wheel; one man, for stealing meal, had a bodkin thrust through his tongue, and was chained to a tree until he starved. Many dug holes in the earth and hid themselves until they famished. So great was the scarcity that they were constrained to eat dogs, cats, rats, and snakes, and one man killed his wife to eat, for which he was burned. Many fed on corpses; and some wished Sir Thomas Smythe on the back of a mare which the Indians had killed and were boiling."

Disheartened, they sought relief in drunkenness. "Dupper's stinking beer" arrived in every vessel, and one captain boasted that with four bottles of wine he would clear the expenses of a whole voyage.

This condition of affairs led to many personal altercations, and George Harrison, in a duel with Richard Stevens, was wounded in the knee, from the effects of which he died in ten days. Such reports from Jamestown only tended to increase the discord of the meetings of the Virginia Company. Sir Francis Nethersole told a friend, "that the factions in the company were as violent as between Guelphs and Ghibelines, and they seldom met but they quarreled. If the society be not dissolved soon, or remodeled, worse effects may follow." The Earl of Warwick and Lord Cavendish, at one meeting, called each other liars.

On the sixteenth of June, 1624, the charter of the company was declared void. Wentworth, writing to his kinsman, the virtuous Christopher Wandesforde, humorously says: "yesterday Virginia patent was overthrown at the King's Bench, so an end of that plantation's savings.

"Methinks I imagine the Quaternity before this have had a meeting of comfort and consolation, stirring up each other to bear it courageously, and Sir Edwin Sandys in the midst of them sadly sighing forth, Oh! the burden of Virginia."

In the place of the old directors, a provisional government was formed by the King, of which Calvert was a member. From the day that Buckingham broke off the negotiations at Madrid, relative to the marriage of Charles, Calvert's position became unpleasant. He had been fully committed to the scheme, he did not dream of its failure, and late in May, 1623, he wrote that "orders are given for all things needful for the reception of the Prince and the Infanta."

When the intelligence reached England that the deep-laid plan had been unsuccessful, he not only suffered from personal disappointment, but with the populace he was an object of obloquy, because an acknowledged leader of what was called the Spanish Party, and therefore it was not politic for the King to appear on terms of great intimacy.

The whole of the year 1624 was one of anxiety for him, as extracts from various letters prove. Early in April, one wrote that Secretary Calvert was in ill health, and talked of resigning his office to Sir Dudley Carleton. A day or two after, it is said "that he is on ill terms with the

King and Prince Charles, and is called to account among other things for detaining letters a year ago, at the request of the French Ambassador." The next month some one thinks, the Secretary does not mean to resign, but by feigning it, to induce the King to give him a larger share of business.

But the letters written to Sir Dudley Carleton, then abroad in the public service, by his son, probably tell the truth. He tells his father that Secretary Calvert proposes to resign on the ground of ill health, and that he is willing to sell the Secretaryship to him for six thousand pounds; that Lord Hollis had offered eight thousand, and Sir John Suckling seven thousand.

Buckingham had not been on good terms with Calvert for some time, and he approved of his proposed resignation, and some whispered if he did not resign he would be displaced.

The summer had now come, and faint in heart and sick in body he retired to his country seat, Thistleworth, where he was cheered by pleasant letters from his constant friend, Wentworth, who was rusticating in Yorkshire.

In a letter dated August the twenty-fourth, 1624, Wentworth alludes to the rumored retirement in these words:

" Since you are like those ancient Romans retired from Court to the harmless delights of Tusculanie,

> 'Ereptus specioso ejus damno,'

like another Æneas from burning Troy * * Believe it, we may not yet admit you a countryman throughout; your neighbors of Thistleworth may tell you one summer is too little to purge away the leaven of a courtier, and it is time that must approve

> Fitque color primo turbati fluminis imbre
> Purgaturque mora,

we must have more trial, more experience, first initiatus, then adultus, lest you might come to spy out our liberty rather than to keep our counsel, to enjoy the contentment and freedom of our life with peace and quietness."

The same month, Calvert receives another letter from him, passages of which are as redolent of country life as a bucolic: "Our harvest is all in, a most fine season to make fish-ponds; our plums all gone and past, peaches, quinces, and grapes almost fully ripe, which will, I trow, hold better relish with a Thistleworth palate, and approve me how to have the skill to serve every man in his right end. These only we countrymen muse of, hoping in such harmless retirements for a just defense from the higher powers, and possessing ourselves in contentment, may, with Dryope in the poet,

> 'Et siqua est pietas, ab acutæ vulnere falcis
> Et pecoris morsu, frondes defendite nostras.'"

Returning to London in the fall, Calvert was once more engaged in his duties as Secretary of State, and found the Court busy in arranging a French match for the Prince. Parliament was adjourned to the month of October by the King, to which Wentworth alludes in these words: "We conclude that the French treaty must first be consummate before such unruly fellows meet in Parliament, lest they might appear as agile against this, as that other Spanish match. * * For is it a small matter, trow you, for poor swains to unwind so dextrously your courtly true love-knots? You think we see nothing, but believe it, you shall find us legislators no fools; albeit you of the Court (for by this time I am sure you have, by a fair retreat from Thistleworth, quit your part of a country life for this year) think to blear our eyes with your sweet balls, and leave us in the suds when you have done. Thus much for the common weal. For your own self, I am right glad for your ague recovered, hoping it will cleanse away all bad-disposed humors."

The relations of Calvert and Buckingham were now more pleasant, but still it was not expedient that the former should continue in the Secretaryship.

Carleton's son informs his father on November the twenty-third, 1624, that "Secretary Conway declares that there was no one whom he should prefer as colleague, but that Calvert was reconciled to Buckingham, who had assured him that he should have the option of refusing any offer made for his place."

Six weeks before James died, the sale of the Secretaryship was effected. An old letter thus announces the intelligence: "Sir Albert Morton is at New Market, and is sworn in, Secretary Calvert giving him the seals for £6000 and an Irish barony either for him or any one who likes it. Young Hungerford is made a baronet by payment, this being the true golden age."[1]

Two weeks after, he went on a journey to Yorkshire, in company with Sir Tobias Matthew, who became a Jesuit in 1617, and was obliged to retire to the Continent, but on his return was received into favor, and knighted in 1623, and afterward devoted himself to poetry and literature.

Archbishop Abbot, a cotemporary, referring to the affair of the resignation, says: "Secretary

---

[1] Chamberlain, in a letter to Sir Dudley Carleton, gives a little different version. He says: "Sir Albert Morton is not yet returned from New Market, though I hear he be sworn, and hath the seals delivered him by Sir George Calvert, who had £3000 of him, and is to have as much more, somewhere, besides an Irish barony for himself, or where he list to bestow it, for his benefit. Young Hungerford is made a baron *en payant;* for this is the true Golden Age, no penny, no *pater noster.*"

Calvert hath never looked merrily since the Prince's coming out of Spain. It was thought that he was much interested in the Spanish affair. A course was taken to rid him of all employments and negotiations.

"This made him discontented; and, as the saying is, 'desperatio facit monachum,' so he apparently turned Papist, which he now professeth, this being the third time he hath been to blame that way. His Majesty, to dismiss him, suffered him to resign his Secretary's place to Sir Albertus Morton, who paid him £3000 for the same, and the King hath made him Baron of Baltimore in Ireland. So he is withdrawn from us, and having bought a ship of 400 tons, he is going to Newfoundland, where he hath a colony."

The effort to sail this year was not successful, for another writes on April the ninth, 1625: "It is said the Lord Baltimore is now a professed Papist, was going to Newfoundland, and is stayed."

It is difficult to tell the precise time of Calvert's conversion to Romanism, but there is reason to suppose that it was a long period before he made open profession. A writer of that era, Bishop Goodman, who had become a Roman Catholic, gives the following account:

"The third man who was thought to gain by the Spanish match, was Secretary Calvert; and as he was the only secretary employed in the

Spanish match, so undoubtedly he did what good offices he could therein for religion's sake, being infinitely addicted to the Roman Catholic faith, having been converted thereunto by Count Gondomar and Count Arundel, whose daughter Secretary Calvert's son had married; and as it was said, the Secretary did actually catechise his own children, so as to ground them in his own religion; and in his best room having an altar set up, with chalice, candlesticks, and all other ornaments, he brought all strangers thither, never concealing anything, as if his whole joy and comfort had been to make open profession of his religion."

While state policy required his removal from the Secretaryship, and was, owing to some stay law, prevented from going to Newfoundland, he was still in favor with Charles the First, and was the next year called from his retirement in Ireland, to be employed at Brussels in a treaty of peace. It was announced by a London correspondent, under date of March the second, 1626–7, "that the talk of divers great commissioners to go over, about a treaty of peace still holds, and Sir George Calvert, sent for out of Ireland for that service, is now come, and on Tuesday rode with the Duke's grace toward the Court."

For some reason he did not go to Brussels, and again was busy in making preparations to visit his colony of Avalon. From his lodgings in the Surry, he wrote to the Secretary of the Duke of Buckingham, on April the seventh, asking him for the speedy dispatch of the warrant for his ships, the Ark of Avalon, one hundred and sixty tons burden, and the George of Plymouth, one hundred and forty tons, to be exempted from the general stay, as Sir Arthur Aston was waiting to sail.

Charles, from the day of his accession, manifested a desire to be "every inch a king." He was restive under the restrictions of Parliament, and raised moneys under the privy seal. His extortions were so large, that a great party, known in distinction from the Court as the Country party, arose. To this Wentworth, as a former member of Yorkshire, at first allied himself, and when the King, under a privy seal, demanded a loan of him, he refused it as unconstitutional.

Calvert, now Lord Baltimore, who was with his whole heart on the side of the King, was distressed at the position of his friend, and urgently wrote: "I have been here now some two or three months, a spectator upon this great scene of State, where I have no part to play; but you have, for which your friends are sorry. It is your enemies, that bring you on the stage, when they have a hope to see you act your own notable harm; and therefore keep yourself off, I beseech you, et redimas te quam queas minimo.

Furnish not your enemies with matter of triumph when, without detriment either to your honor or conscience, you may give them the foil if you will; and remember the old tale of the rain that fell upon all the world except two that kept themselves in a cellar, and how sorry they were afterward for their providence. * * * So neither forfeit your own, nor by your example prejudice the common right of the subject."

During the latter part of May, Lord Baltimore obtained the long-desired leave, to visit his possessions in Newfoundland.

He went not as a religious exile, nor as a curiosity seeker, but to save his investments if possible. Frankly he tells a friend: "I must either go and settle it in better order, or else give it over, and lose all the charges I have been at hitherto for other men to build their fortunes upon.

"And I had rather be esteemed a fool by some for the hazard of one month's journey, than to prove myself one certainly for six years by past, if the business be now lost for the want of a little pains and care."

Three or four days before his departure, he made another strong appeal to Wentworth to yield to the King's demands: "I should say much more to you were you here, which is not fit for paper; but never put off the matter of your appearance here, for God's sake; but send your money into the collector's without more ado.

"At Michaelmas I hope to be with you, God willing. In the mean time, I shall be in great fear that your too much fortitude will draw upon you suddenly a misfortune which your heart may perhaps endure, but the rest of your body will ill suffer. * * * * The conquering way sometimes is yielding, and so is it, I conceive, in this particular of yours, when you shall both conquer your own passions and vex your enemies, who desire nothing more than your resistance."

These earnest, loving words, touched the impulsive Wentworth, and in a few weeks he deserted the Country and joined the Court party. Pym, who had been intimate with him, was astounded, and made a prophetic speech: "Though you leave us now, I will never leave you, while your head is upon your shoulders."

Parliament was dissolved in June, the twenty-sixth, and on the fourteenth of next month Wentworth was rewarded with a baronetcy, with the expectation of further honors, which rapidly followed.

Before Wentworth deserted the Country party, Lord Baltimore had departed for Newfoundland in a ship of three hundred tons and twenty-four guns, and arrived at the settlement of Ferryland about the twenty-third of July. The companions of his journey were Longvyll and Anthony Smith, two Seminary priests. Robert

Hayman,[1] who was Governor of Newfoundland and a bigoted Protestant, composed a quodlibet on the occasion of his arrival:

> "Great Sheba's wise queen travel'd far to see
> Whether the truth did with report agree;
> You, by report persuaded, laid out much,
> Then wisely came to see if it were such;
> You came and saw, admired what you had seen
> With like success as the wise Sheba queen.
> If every sharer here would take like pain,
> This land would soon be peopled to their gain."

After remaining a few months, he returned to England, taking the priest Longvyll with him. During the spring of 1628, he sailed a second time with his family, a priest named Hacket, and others, about forty in all. During the summer, he was obliged to contend with many difficulties, and found no place that was a "Heart's Content." In a letter from Ferryland, written on the twenty-fifth of August, he pours forth his troubles to the Duke of Buckingham:

"The King once told him that he wrote as fair a hand to look upon afar off as any man in England; but that when any one came near they

---

[1] Hayman was educated at Exeter College, Oxford, and then studied law. But the courts of the Muses were more attractive than those of Lincoln's Inn, and his associates were Ben Jonson, and Owen, the Epigrammatist. At the age of forty he was appointed Governor of a Newfoundland plantation, and there composed his Quodlibets, which were published in London in 1628.

were not able to read a word. He then got a dispensation to use another man's, for which he is thankful, as writing is a great pain to him now. Owes an account of his proceedings in this plantation to the Duke, since it was under his Grace's patronage that he went out. He came to build and set and sow, but he has fallen to fighting with Frenchmen."

The details of the sea-fight are then given. De la Rade, with three ships and four hundred men, "many of them gentlemen of quality, la fleur de la jeunesse de Normandye," had appeared off the fishing banks and captured several vessels.

Lord Baltimore sent two ships in pursuit, one carrying twenty-four guns. Upon their approach, the French in alarm dropped their captures, and the English took six prizes and sixty-seven prisoners, which Baltimore had to support all the summer. The longer he continued at Ferryland the less hopeful he became, and this summer Hayman wrote another quodlibet in reference to Baltimore's meditated return from the colony:

"Your honor, hath got your honor in your day;
It is my honor you my verses praise.
O! let your honor cheerfully go on,
End well your well-begun plantation.
This holy, hopeful work you have half-done,
For, best of any, you have well begun.
If you give over what hath so well sped,
Your solid wisdom will be questioned."

During the autumn of 1628, he appears to have sent over Leonard Calvert to look after the prizes and interests of the colony, and he humbly petitions that he may have a share in the prizes, that had been taken from the French by the ships Benediction and Victory, and that a letter of marque ante-dated might be issued, so that he may receive his proportion. His brother-in-law, Will. Peasley, also presents his petition to the Lords of the Admiralty, asking for the use of the ship St. Claude for preservation of the King's rights and many subjects in Newfoundland.

The Rev. Erasmus Sturton, who was the Protestant minister at Ferryland, in consequence of some dissatisfaction, left there on the twenty-sixth of August, and the following October, at Plymouth, England, made complaint of the proselyting efforts of the priests who had accompanied Baltimore. He stated, that every Sunday mass and all the ceremonies of the Church were performed, and that the child of one William Pool, a Protestant, was baptized into the Church of Rome, contrary to the will of his father.

In the spring of the year 1629, the St. Claude, under a letter of marque, with Leonard Calvert as supercargo, sailed for Newfoundland, and on August the nineteenth, in a letter to the King, written at Ferryland, Baltimore "gives thanks upon his knees for the loan of a fair ship;" complains of the calumny and malice of those who seek to make him appear foul in his Majesty's eyes, and of the slanderous reports raised at Plymouth last winter by an audacious man,[1] who was banished the colony for his misdeeds; has met with difficulties in this place no longer to be resisted, and is forced to shift to some warmer climate of the New World, where the winters are shorter and less rigorous; speaks of the severity of the weather from October to May, both land and sea frozen the greatest part of the time. "His house has been a hospital all the winter; of one hundred persons, fifty sick at one time, he being one; also nine or ten have died. His strength is much decayed; but his inclination carries him naturally to proceedings in plantations." He

---

[1] Sturton became the Chaplain of Lord Anglesea. Hayman seems to have liked him, as he dedicated the following "To my Reverend, kind friend Erasmus Sturton, Preacher of the Word of God and Parson of Ferryland, in the Province of Avalon, in Newfoundland:

"No man should be more welcome to this place
Than such as you, Angel of peace and grace;
As you were sent here by the Lord's command,
Be you the blest Apostle of this land;
To Infidels do you evangelize,
Making those that are rude sober and wise.
I pray the Lord, that did you hither send,
Our cursings, swearing, jouring[1] mend."

---

[1] Jouring, a provincialism for murmuring.

then requests a grant of a precinct of land in Virginia, where he wishes to remove with some forty persons, with such privileges as King James granted to him in Newfoundland. Soon after this, without waiting a reply from the King, he sent his children to England, and with his lady visited Virginia. Upon his arrival at Jamestown, the Governor (West) and Council, composed of William Clayborne and others, called him before them and inquired what his purpose was, being Governor of another plantation, to abandon that and come thus to Virginia. He replied that he came to plant and dwell. "Very willingly, my Lord," they answered, "if your Lordship will do what we have done and what your duty is to do."

They then administered the oath of allegiance, which he cheerfully took, but refused that of supremacy. Whereupon they told him that they dared not admit any man into their settlement who would not acknowledge all the prerogatives of his Majesty, and asked him to depart in the next ship. Leaving his lady in Virginia, he hastened to England, to find that on November the twenty-second the King, in a letter dated "White-Hall," had written to him that, "Seeing his plantation in Newfoundland has not answered expectations, that he is in pursuit of new countries, and weighing that men of his condition and breeding are fitter for other employments than the framing of new plantations, which commonly have rugged and laborious beginnings, the King has thought fit to advise him to desist from further prosecuting his designs, and to return to his native country, where he shall enjoy such respect as his former services and later endeavors justly deserve."

A letter written by Mead, of Christ College, to Sir Martin Stuteville, thus alludes to these events: "My Lord Baltimore, alias Sir George Calvert, being weary of his intolerable plantation at Newfoundland, where he hath found between eight and nine months winter, and upon the land nothing but rocks, lakes or morasses like bogs, which one might thrust a spike down to the butt-head, for so Mr. James, Sir Robert Cotton's library-keeper,[1] who was sent minister thither some nine years ago, describes the place; his

[1] Richard James was born in 1608, and was a very young man when in Newfoundland, and soon returned to England. Educated at Oxford, he proved a very good scholar, and although a clergyman by profession, he was looked upon as a trifler and jester. He published several works and poems. Some have asserted that he was an illegitimate son of Sir Robert Cotton. He was that gentleman's librarian, and without permission, lent a manuscript written by Dudley, an English nobleman living in Italy, the contents of which being made public, led to Cotton's arrest, and broke his heart. James died in 1638, at the house of Sir Thomas Cotton, a son of Sir Robert. (See Athenæ Oxonienses, and Gentleman's Magazine, 1767 and 1768.)

Lordship this last summer sent home all his children into England, and went with his lady into Virginia."

Governor John Pott, Samuel Matthews, Roger Smyth, and William Clayborne remonstrated with the Privy Council, in behalf of the Colony of Virginia, relative to Baltimore's visit. In a communication of November the thirteenth, they state: "That about the beginning of October last Lord Baltimore arrived in Virginia, from his plantation in Newfoundland, with intention, as they are informed, to plant to the southward, but has since seemed willing to reside with his family at this place. He, and some of his followers, being of the Romish religion, utterly refused to take the oaths of supremacy and allegiance, tendered to them according to instructions received from King James. As they have been made happy in the freedom of their religion, they implore that, as heretofore, no Papists may be suffered to settle among them."

Notwithstanding the rude treatment he had met in Virginia, the King was friendly, for in December Baltimore not only asks for a letter from the Privy Council to the Governor of Virginia in behalf of his lady still there, to aid her in returning to England, but also prays for a grant of a portion of land in Virginia, *the King having given him leave to choose a part.*

The first winter after Baltimore's return, a

fresh interest was created in the New World, by the arrival of a chief, and his wife and son, from Nova Scotia. They were treated with much attention, particularly by Lord Poulet, in Somersetshire, and Lady Poulet took the chief's wife up to London and presented her with a necklace and diamond.

Pory, the celebrated scholar and traveler, and at one time Secretary of the Colony of Virginia, in a letter to Joseph Mead, chaplain of Archbishop Laud, written on February the twelfth, 1629–30, makes rather a satirical allusion to Lord Baltimore's attempt to induce settlement in his plantations. His words are:

"Now for the King, Queen, and Prince of Newfoundland; they have no relation to Virginia, nor to my Lord Baltimore's being there, who, though his Lordship is extolling that country to the skies, yet he is preparing a bark to send to fetch his lady and servants from thence, because the King will not permit him to go back again. And for that King and Prince so much talked of, I hold them of no great importance against the French, by reason of the paucity of their subjects, who if they be one hundred men, women, and children, it is a great matter in that horrid region. But if the principal patentee of that flourishing new kingdom can, by making show and ostentation of them, effect his project of creating an order of baronets of New Scotland,[1] who, for £500, shall have precedence of all Scotch and Irish baronets, of all English also of a future creation; shall have the privilege of being free from arrests; shall have one thousand acres of land in that tract, and a ribbon, with an order hanging thereto, for distinction's sake, then I will extol him for his wit and industry."

John Harvey, the Governor of Virginia, appointed by King Charles, after the death of Yeardley, arrived in Jamestown early in 1630, and he seems to have brought to justice those that had been rude to Lord Baltimore at the time of his visit. A record of March the twenty-fifth, 1630, reads: "Thomas Tindall to be pilloried two hours for giving my Lord Baltimore the lie, and threatening to knock him down."[2]

No one welcomed back Baltimore more cordially than Charles, and a letter written from the Castle Yard on August the twelfth, 1630, to his old friend, Lord Wentworth, shows that his relations with the Court were very pleasant: "All here at home are as your Lordship left us, saving only, that the Prince's nurse is very sick of a fever, and for that cause another is in her room. The Prince himself, thanks be to God, is very

---

[1] Sir W. Alexander, Secretary of State for Scotland, and called by James "his philosophic poet," was the patentee of New Scotland, or Nova Scotia, and he sold baronetcies, with heraldic medals, but it proved a poor speculation.

[2] Hening's Statutes, vol. i.

well, and so are the King and Queen; and, as I heard this very day, the Queen discovered to be with child again; but that, being yet but women's news, is not to be talked till everybody may see it. I pray God it be true."[1]

During the spring of this year Francis West, who had been Governor, William Clayborne, Secretary, and William Tucker, one of the Council of Virginia, were in London resisting the planting of a new colony within the limits of the settled parts of Virginia.

Baltimore received from Charles the First, several tokens of good will. On March the thirty-first a warrant was issued "to pay to George Lord Baltimore £2000, to be deducted out of the increase of subsidy on raw silk importation;" and on the third of October, on condition of resigning pension previously granted, a pension of £1000 annually was substituted.

A few days after this, his intimate friend Wentworth lost his second wife Arabella, the beautiful daughter of Earl Clare, which elicited from Baltimore a letter of condolence, imbued with the sublime teachings of Christianity:

My Lord:

Were not my occasions such as necessarily keep me here at this time, I would not send let-

---

[1] The "women's news" proved correct. The Princess Mary was born May 4, 1631.

ters, but fly to you myself, with all the speed I could, to express my own grief, and to take part of yours, which I know is exceedingly great, for the loss of so noble a lady, so virtuous and loving a wife.

There are few perhaps can judge of it better than I, who have been myself a long time a man of sorrows. But all things, my Lord, in this world pass away; statutum est, wife, children, honor, wealth, friends, and what else is dear to flesh and blood; they are but lent us till God please to call for them back again, that we may not esteem anything our own, or set our hearts upon anything but Him alone, who only remains forever.

I beseech his Almighty Goodness to grant that your Lordship may, for his sake, bear this great cross with meekness and patience, whose only Son, our dear Lord and Saviour, bore a greater for you; and to consider that these humiliations, though they be very bitter, yet are they sovereign medicines, ministered unto us by our Heavenly Physician, to cure the sickness of our Souls, if the fault be not ours.

Good my Lord! bear with this excess of zeal in a friend, whose great affection to you transports him to dwell longer upon this melancholy theme, than is needful to your Lordship, whose own wisdom, assisted with God's grace, I hope suggests unto you these and better resolutions, than I can offer to your remembrance. All I have to say more, is but this, that I humbly and heartily pray you so to dispose of yourself and your affairs (the rite being done to that noble creature) so as to be able to remove, as soon as conveniently you may, from those parts where so many things represent themselves unto you, as to make your wound bleed afresh; and let us have you here, where the gracious welcome of your Master, the conversation of your friends, and variety of businesses, may divert your thoughts the sooner from sad objects, the continuance whereof will but endanger your health, on which depends the welfare of your children, the comfort of your friends, and many other good things, for which I hope God will reserve you, to whose divine favor I humbly recommend you, and remain,

Your Lordship's

Most affectionate and faithful servant,

GEO. BALTIMORE.

From my Lodgings in
LINCOLN'S INN FIELDS, October 11, 1631.

Baltimore had not the slightest sympathy with popular government, and he viewed with displeasure the firm and manly opposition of the Parliament to the arrogant demands of the King.

Finding but little comfort where the popular

will was beginning to control, and being a favorite of King Charles, his leisure hours were occupied in writing a charter for a new plantation, in which he would be made sole proprietor, with little less than regal power, far above the will of the people, and at the same time contain provisions that would be attractive to settlers, as well as pecuniarily profitable to himself.

After it was prepared, it was submitted to and approved by Charles the First. Having left a blank for the name of the proposed colony, Charles inserted Terra Mariæ, in honor of his French wife, Queen Mary, as Henrietta was frequently called. Ogilby says, that had not the King used his privilege of giving a name, it was Baltimore's intention to have called the proposed new settlement, Crescentia.

An analysis of the charter proves it to be destitute of a single democratic element. By it he and his heirs were created true and absolute Lords and Proprietaries of the region; with free, full, and absolute power to ordain, make, and enact laws, with the advice, assent, and approbation of the freemen of the province, and with authority to appoint all judges, justices, and constables.

The freemen could only meet in Assembly with his permission, and the eighth section expressly provides that he may make wholesome ordinances from time to time, to be kept and observed, on the ground that it might be necessary, before the freeholders of said province could be convened for the purpose. As he could not, by the laws of England, make the Church of Rome the established Church, a check was held on all religious denominations, by securing the patronage of all churches that should happen to be built.[1]

Desiring to be just, and to promote what he thought were the best interests of the colonists, it was far from his intention that they should molest him, as the Parliament were troubling Charles, and as the democratic Virginia Assembly had annoyed him and others.

Believing an aristocracy to be a desirable element in society, the first part of the fourteenth section of the charter reads thus:

"Moreover, lest in so remote and far distant a region, every access to honors and dignities may seem to be precluded, and utterly barred to

---

[1] Chalmers says: "The rights of the Parliament were carefully alluded to, but the prerogatives of the Crown and the rights of the nation were in a great measure overlooked and forgotten."

The copy of the Annals which I have used in my investigations is the presentation copy to Lord Hailes, on a leaf of which, in the author's handwriting, is the following:

"Sir John Dalrymple, Bart., the author, presents these Annals, which had never been written but for his advice, the only merit of which is owing to his kindness, as an evidence of the consideration and gratitude of the author."

men well born, who are preparing to engage in the present expedition, and desirous of deserving well both in peace and war, of us and our kingdoms; for this cause, we do give free and plenary power to the aforesaid now Baron of Baltimore, and to his heirs and assigns, to confer favors, rewards, and honors upon such subjects, inhabiting within the province aforesaid, as shall be well deserving, and to adorn them with whatever titles and dignities they shall appoint."

Before the grant was formally made out, Baltimore became sick, and after sending a farewell message to his long tried friend Wentworth, he died on April the thirteenth, 1632, and was buried in the chancel of St. Dunstan's West, London.[1]

---

[1] George Calvert married Anne, daughter of George Mynne, who died in August, 1622, who had given birth to ten children before he became Secretary. Burke, in his "Extinct Peerage," mentions but four:

Cecil, his successor.

Leonard, Governor of Maryland.

Anna, wife of William Peasley, Esq.

Grace, wife of Sir Robert Talbot, of County Kildare, Ireland.

George, who accompanied Leonard to America, it is thought died in Virginia.

The lady who accompanied him to Newfoundland and Virginia, does not appear to have been his wife, and Stuyvesant says that Governor Philip Calvert was an illegitimate son.

CHAPTER SECOND.

CECILIUS BALTIMORE, AND FORMATIVE PERIOD OF THE COLONY.

THREE months after the remains of the first Lord Baltimore were deposited in the chancel of St. Dunstan's, London, the patent that had been promised to him was formally issued in the name of Cecilius, his son and successor.

By its provisions he was empowered to transport, by his own industry and experience, a numerous colony of the English nation, to "*a country hitherto uncultivated,* extending from Watkin's Point, near the River Wigho [Pocomoke], unto that part of the Bay of Delaware on the north which lieth under the fortieth degree of north latitude, where New England is terminated." The charter granted by Charles, in the sixth section adds: "That the aforesaid region may be eminently distinguished, above all other regions of that territory, and decorated with more ample titles, know ye, that WE, of our more special grace, have thought fit that the said region and islands be united into a PROVINCE, and nominate the same MARYLAND, by which name we will that it shall from henceforth be called."

Hayman, in his book of Quodlibets, published in London in 1628, alludes to the Newfoundland plantation of Lord Baltimore in these lines:

> "Your's is a holy, just plantation,
> And not a jostling supplantation."

The same could scarcely be said of the Maryland Plantation, for as soon as the charter was issued it was felt by many to be partial and arbitrary.[1]

Members of the old Virginia Company immediately offered objections, on the grounds of law, equity, and inconvenience, which were subsequently followed by a remonstrance of the

---

[1] Kent and Palmer's Isle had already been occupied by English settlers. Palmer's Isle, at the mouth of the Susquehanna, was probably named after Edward Palmer, of Leamington, Gloucester County, England. Camden says he was "a curious and diligent antiquary." He was an uncle of Sir Thomas Overbury.

Fuller, in his "Worthies," says: "His plenteous estate afforded him opportunity to put forward the ingenuity, implanted by nature, for the public good, resolving to erect an academy in Virginia. In order whereunto he purchased an island, called Palmer's Island unto this day, but in pursuance thereof was at many thousand pounds expense, some instruments employed therein not discharging the trust reposed in them with corresponding fidelity. He was transplanted to another world, leaving to posterity the monument of his worthy but unfinished intention. This Edward Palmer died in London about 1625."

planters of Virginia. But the Baltimore influence could not be overthrown in a Privy Council where he was esteemed, and a powerful member of which was Wentworth, an old family friend, and on July the third, 1633, it was decided by them that Baltimore should not be disturbed, and a few days after a letter was written to the Governor and Council of Virginia, stating that Lord Baltimore intended to transport a number of persons "to that part called Maryland, which we have given him," and they are directed to give him friendly help and assistance in furtherance of his undertaking.

Cecil Baltimore now earnestly labored to collect a colony for embarkation, but he found his pathway filled with the thorns planted by opponents.

After the "Ark," a ship of four hundred tons, and the "Dove," a pinnace of fifty tons, were purchased, it was whispered that he designed to carry nuns and soldiers to Spain; then, after they had sailed, it was reported that they had not complied with the custom-house regulations, and Secretary Coke wrote to Admiral Pennington, that the Ark of London, Richard Lowe, master, carrying men for Lord Baltimore to his new plantation "in or about New England," had sailed from Gravesend contrary to orders, the company in charge of Captain Winter not having taken the oath of allegiance.

The vessels were immediately pursued and brought back, and on the thirtieth of October license was granted for the Ark and Dove to go to Maryland, the oath having been administered to the passengers.

Some bills having been unsettled, complaint was made against Lord Baltimore and his deputy, Gabriel Hawley.

It set forth, that Hawley billeted men and women for Maryland, at twelve pence a day, in the houses of the complainants, and took them away without paying for their entertainment, amounting to about sixty pounds; and that Lord Baltimore refers them to Hawley, now a prisoner in the Fleet, and they ask that Lord Baltimore, whose ship is ready to sail, may be ordered to give satisfaction.

Sir John Wostenholme and others also declared, that they had been at great charge in settling an island, by them named the Isle of Kent, and prayed that they might enjoy free trade, and that Lord Baltimore might settle in some other place.

But toward the last of November all difficulties were surmounted, and they reached Cowes, in the Isle of Wight, where probably the Jesuits came on board. On the twenty-second of November they weighed anchor, and steered for the New World. The gentlemen, not twenty in number, were on board of the Dove, Captain Winter in command;

and the laboring men were stowed away in the Ark, under the charge of Captain Richard Lowe.[1]

The colony was not religious, but commercial, in its aims. The members thereof were Protestants and Roman Catholics.

Among the few gentlemen of the colony were Leonard Calvert, aged twenty-six years, and George, a younger brother, who seems to have lived in Virginia, and died there about the year 1667.[2] The two councillors were Thomas Cornwallis and Jerome Hawley. The former became a useful and valuable citizen of the province, and was probably the son of Sir Thomas Cornwallis. Jerome Hawley had been one of the

---

[1] Cecilius Baltimore, in a letter to Wentworth, written from Odiham, January 10th, 1633-4, says:

"I have, by the help of some of your Lordship's good friends and mine, overcome these difficulties, and sent a hopeful colony into Maryland, with a fair and favorable expectation of good success; however, without any danger of any great prejudice unto myself in respect that many others are joined with me in the adventure. There are two of my brothers gone, with *very near twenty* other gentlemen of very good fashion, and *three hundred laboring men*, well provided in all things."—*Strafford's Dispatches and Letters*, vol. i.

[2] Governor Maverick, of Massachusetts, wrote in October, 1667:

"That there had been a hurricane in Virginia, and it was said that Lord Baltimore's son had died."—*N. Y. Col. Documents.*

gentlemen sewers of Queen Henrietta Maria, and was soon the Treasurer of the Colony of Virginia, where he died. Four, at least, of the few remaining gentlemen were sons of titled Englishmen, and members of old Roman Catholic families.[1] The laboring men on board of the Ark were largely Protestant, for Father White, in his journal, says that, of twelve that died on the passage to America, only two were Roman Catholics.

Deeply interested in the propagation of religion, under the forms Baltimore approved, he dispatched with the colonists Fathers Andrew White and John Altham, *alias* Gravener, of the Society of Jesus, with John Knowles and Thomas Gervase as assistants, two of whom appear on the

---

1 In "A Relation of Maryland," published in 1635, republished in 1865, is a list of "very near twenty gentlemen," who were with the first colony :

Leonard Calvert, George Calvert, his Lordship's brothers.

Jerome Hawley, Esq., Thomas Cornwallis, Esq., Commissioners.

Richard Gerard, son of Sir Thomas Gerard, K. B.

Edward Wintour, Frederick Wintour, sons of Lady Anne Wintour.

Henry Wiseman, son of Sir Thomas Wiseman, Bart.

John Saunders, Thomas Dorrel, Edward Cranfield, Captain John Hill, Henry Green, John Medcalf, Nicholas Fairfax, William Saire, John Baxter.

Fairfax died at sea.

catalogue of Jesuits of Clerkenwell College, that was in 1627 broken up.[1]

After tarrying twenty days at the Barbadoes, and fourteen at St. Christopher's, Leonard Calvert and party arrived on the twenty-fourth of February at Point Comfort, Va. Visiting Governor Harvey, at Jamestown, they did not leave that point until the third of March. On the fifth they were at the mouth of the Potomac, and then ascending fourteen leagues, they came to St. George Isle, and anchored at "an island near unto it which they called S. Clements," where they set up a cross, and took possession of this country "for our Saviour and for our Sovereign Lord the King of England," with ceremonies very similar to those which a poet[2] has described in connection with the planting of Christianity in Great Britain:

> "In the bright
> Fringe of the living sea, that came and went,
> Tapping its planks, a great ship sideways lay;
> And o'er the sands a grave procession passed,
> Melodious with many a chanting voice.
> Nor spear, nor buckler had these foreign men;
> Each wore a snowy robe, that downward flowed;

---

[1] These names are taken from the Catalogue of Clerkenwell College, in the Camden Soc. Publications:

"Jōes Gravenerius.

"Thomas Gervasii.

"Philippus Fisherus, *alias* Musket."

Fisher was at St. Mary's in 1639.

[2] Alex. Smith, in "Edwin of Deira."

Fair in the front a silver cross they bore,
A painted Saviour floated in the wind;
The chanting voices, as they rose and fell,
Hallowed the rude sea air."

Leaving the Ark at the island, Calvert in his pinnace ascended the river as far as "Paschatoway," when he met Captain Henry Fleet,[1] an Englishman who had lived many years among the Indians. Descending the river again with Fleet as a guide, he was conducted up a small tributary to the Indian village of Yoacomaco, which, being well situated, was purchased from the Indians, and on the twenty-seventh of March, 1634, the Governor took possession, and named the place Saint Mary's. Three days after the Ark, with the two pinnaces, came up from the island, and the next day they began to build a block and store-house, the colonists living on board of the ships until they were completed.

A few days subsequent Governor Harvey, of Virginia, visited the infant settlement.

They found the country well stored with corn,

---

1 The Admiralty, on July 10, 1634, received the following petition of George Griffith & Co., proprietors of the ship Warwick, of London:

"Three years past they set forth a ship to New England and Virginia, for trade and discovery, and appointed Henry Fleet their factor, with commission to return within one year; but, by authority of Sir John Harvey, Governor of Virginia, Fleet has restrained the vessel, and profits to the petitioners' great loss."—*Col. State Papers, Col. Ser.*, p. 184.

and the Indian women taught them how to make it into bread. The ground being prepared for cultivation, they made gardens, and planted English seeds of all sorts, and the summer proved very favorable for vegetation.

As soon as the plentiful harvest of the first season was over, finding that, with what they had purchased from the Indians, they had more corn than was needed for the coming winter, the little Dove, a pinnace as dear to the descendants of Roman Catholics as the Mayflower is to the children of Puritans in America, sailed from Saint Mary for Boston, laden with grain, and for the purpose of cultivating friendly relations with the Colony of Massachusetts, over which the gentle and dignified Winthrop presided, and whose descendants to this day have maintained a character for personal bravery and scholarly culture.

From the time that the Dove first appeared in the harbor of Boston, vessels constantly coasted from colony to colony, exchanging products.

The crew at the time of their visit did not behave very well. It was a rule of the port that all vessels should anchor below the fort; also that no one should land without a permit, and that all should return to their ships by sunset.

The sailors of the Maryland pinnace did not like thus to be "cabined, cribbed, and confined," and leaning over the side of the ship, they gave vent to their animal spirits by shouting nicknames to the Puritans on shore, calling them the "brethren," and the "members," and, saith the grave Winthrop in his journal, "did curse and swear most horribly, and use threatening speeches." These acts caused virtuous indignation among the "solid men of Boston." The Governor, his assistants, and the divines were all consulted, and it was decided that an example ought to be made of the evil-doers; but, as the sailors were not on land, the knotty question arose, how shall we obtain them from the vessel? The Gordian knot was at last cut, by arresting the innocent supercargo, who happened to be on shore, and causing him to give bail for the appearance of the offenders on the day fixed for trial.

When the men of the sea were brought to court, a greater difficulty arose, for no one could positively swear as to the identity of the man or men who had jeered and blasphemed, and the case was therefore dismissed, and a letter written to the captain, requesting him to bring among them "no more such disorderly persons."

These prejudices against Puritans were not entirely confined to the mariners of the Maryland province. In the beautiful narrative of Father White's labors among the Piscataways, not many miles below the site of the City of

Washington, he gives a reason for the affection of a chief of that tribe for him and his colleagues.

The savage told him that he had a dream, in which he saw his deceased father worshiping a dark and hideous God; at a little distance was a most ludicrous demon, accompanied by a settler named Snow, "an obstinate heretic from England;" at length Governor Calvert and Father White appeared, in the company of a beautiful God of exceeding whiteness, who with gentleness beckoned to him; and since that vision he had been drawn by cords of love toward the black robes.

According to their prejudices, those who peruse this story will call it a wonderful Providence, an Indian superstition, a Jesuit fiction, or will say, "credat Judæus Appella;" but whatever the conclusion, it proves that some one had impressed the untutored savage with the belief that those who were not Roman Catholics were heretics.

But while religious differences existed, Leonard Calvert, as governor of the province, seemed to protect all in their conscientious scruples, for had he oppressed them, they would have crossed the river to Virginia, where settlers were so much needed, and the enemies of the colony would have triumphed.

The first Protestant colonists were principally

indented white servants and poor young men who came to seek their fortunes. They had no guide of their faith furnished by the Proprietor for the cure of their souls, but in their chests a few books had been placed by anxious friends and parents, that had proved sources of comfort in hours of doubt, temptation, and loneliness.

Thomas Cornwallis, a councillor of the province, had a number of white servants under the care of an overseer, named William Lewis. One day, in the year 1638, these servants were listening to the reading of sermons written by the eloquent Puritan divine, known in England as the "silver-tongued Smith,"[1] when the overseer in a rage said that "the book came from the devil, as all lies did, and that he that wrote it was an instrument of the devil, and that they should not keep nor read such books." Christopher Carroll and others of the aggrieved, complained of this abuse to the civil authorities, and to the credit of the Governor and Council, Lewis was found guilty of an offensive and indiscreet speech, and fined five hundred pounds of tobacco.

Late in the month of November, of the year 1637, John Lewger, the most remarkable man of any that had hitherto arrived, appeared at Saint Mary. There came with him Ann, his wife, his son John, nine years of age, three male and three

---

1 Wood's Athenæ Oxonienses.

female servants, and a boy, Robert, twelve years old.

On the previous fifteenth of April, he had been commissioned in London as secretary of the province, and collector and receiver of all his Lordship's rents and revenues. Subsequently he was privy councillor, attorney-general, and judge of all causes testamentary and matrimonial.

He had been a college friend of Cecil Baltimore at Oxford,[1] a commoner of Trinity College in 1616, and received the degree of Master of Arts in 1622, and was made Bachelor of Divinity at the same time as Phil. Nye, afterward prominent in the Westminster Assembly of theologians.

In 1632 he was a minister of the Church of England, in Essex, but under the influence of the acute disputant Will. Chillingworth, he became a Roman Catholic, and by a singular coincidence the proselyter, who was a god-son of Bishop Laud, very soon returned to the Church of England, and became the author of the oft-quoted sentence: "The Bible, and that only is the religion of Protestants, and every one, by making use of the helps and assistances that God had placed in his hands, must learn and understand it for himself as well as he can."

---

[1] Wood's Athenæ Oxonienses.

Lewger was chagrined when he learned that Chillingworth had reverted, but the latter answered his wrath in a kind letter, entitled "Reasons against Popery, in a letter from Mr. Wm. Chillingworth to his friend Mr. Lewger, persuading him to return to his mother, the Church of England, from the corrupt Church of Rome."

The letter somewhat appeased Lewger, and he had a conference with his old friend, in the presence of Bishops Skinner and Sheldon.

Deprived of his benefice, a married man, with no means of support, Cecil Baltimore made him Secretary of Maryland, and sent him to assist his brother Leonard. In the provincial assemblies he was influential, and in that of 1639 he voted twelve proxies.

In this connection it is appropriate to allude to the name of Thomas Copley, Esq., which appears in the earliest records of the province.

He entered lands for Fathers White and Altham, and thirty others, in 1635, one of whom was "Francisco, a mulatto," brought in by Father White, and the first slave in the colony of which there is any notice. Copley appears to have been the land agent for the Jesuit fathers, as another record says: "Thomas Copley, Esq., demandeth four thousand acres of land, due by conditions of plantation, for transporting into this province himself and twenty able men, at his own charge, to plant and inhabit in the year 1637."

On the thirteenth of May, 1638, there was also entered "for Mr. Thomas Copley, one hundred weight of beaver, traded for with the Indians."[1]

As late as 1650, members of the Roman Catholic Church bequeathed slight testimonials to the Rev. Thomas Copley, and in some missionary letters he is called Father Copley. This gentleman may have been the Father Copley[2] who, when domestic chaplain of Lord Montague, fell in love with the nursery-maid, and forgetting his vows, was married, and of course, as long as his wife lived, could only serve in secular affairs.

On the fifth of July, 1640, Father White, in the presence of his colleague, Altham, alias Gravener, Governor Calvert, Secretary Lewger, and others, baptized a Piscataway chief, with his wife and daughter. The chief was christened Charles, the wife Mary, and the child Anna, as complimentary to the royal family of Engand.

On the afternoon of the same day the chief was married according to the rites of the Church of Rome, and a cross was planted commemorative of the event, the priests chanting the litany; while Calvert, Lewger, and others followed in solemn procession.

---

[1] Bozman.

[2] Letter of John Chamberlain to Sir Dudley Carleton, in "Court and Times of James the First."

Tanner, in his "Gesta Prœclara," published nigh two centuries ago, across the seas, in the far distant City of Prague, gives a rude engraving of the baptismal scene;[1] but this and the marriage ceremony remain yet to be colored on canvas or embalmed in poetry by some American Weir or Longfellow.

The journal of the early Jesuit mission in Maryland abounds in religious sentiment. Shortly after the marriage of the chief, Father Altham died on Kent Island, and White, writing to Europe, said: "Those who are sent need not fear lest the means of support be wanting, for He who clothes the lilies and feeds the birds of the air, will not suffer those who are laboring to extend his kingdom, to be destitute of necessary sustenance."

Brock, whose real name was Morgan, and who died July the fifth, 1641, wrote: "For my part, I would rather, laboring in the conversion of the Indians, expire on the bare ground, deprived of all human succor, and perishing from hunger, than ever think of abandoning the holy work of God for fear of want."

They were trained to be soldiers of the cross; they enjoyed the canoe voyage, camping in the open air, and their scanty fare, more than the pampered children of luxury the choicest delicacies. "With this present comfort," one said,

---

[1] Shea's Cath. Missions.

"God now imparts to us a foretaste of what he is about to give to those that live faithfully in this life, and mitigating all hardship with a degree of pleasantness, so that his Divine Majesty appears to be present with us in an external manner."

In 1639, the Fathers were settled in places widely distant: Fisher was at St. Mary; Brock at Mattapany on the Patuxent, two miles from its mouth; Altham at Kent Island, sixty miles from St. Mary; and White one hundred and twenty miles distant, perhaps at Clayborne's old trading post near the mouth of the Susquehanna.

On the twelfth of December, 1635, Governor Harvey, of Virginia, appeared before the Privy Council of England to answer certain questions. He admitted that one Rabnet, of Maryland, had been arrested in Virginia for saying that it was lawful and meritorious to kill a heretic king, and that a Rev. Mr. Williams was ready to give testimony; but he refused the testimony because he had married two persons without a license.

It was charged that Governor Harvey countenanced the religion in Maryland, and that Mr. Hawley, in the midst of the mass, said that he was come to plant the Romish religion in Maryland. This was denied; but both admitted that there was public mass in that colony.[1]

---

[1] Cal. State Papers, Domestic Series.

On the twenty-second of March, 1642, a petition was presented to the Assemby of Maryland in behalf of the Protestant Catholics by David Wickliff, complaining of Surgeon Thomas Gerard, who came into the colony in 1638, and owner of St. Clement's manor, for taking away the key and books of their chapel. In settlements without ministers, it was customary in those days to fasten to a desk in a chapel the Bible, and a few valuable religious books, which the devout could open and read.

Doctor Gerard was brought to trial, and, after patient hearing, it was adjudged that he should bring back the key and books, and pay a fine of five hundred pounds of tobacco toward the maintenance of the first Protestant minister that should arrive. The term Protestant Catholic was not unusual in that age. The Jesuit father, Fitz-Herbert, when arraigned in the colony for an alleged offense, argued that in the province every church "professing to believe in God the Father, Son, and Holy Ghost, was accounted Holy Church,"[1] and therefore the inhabitants distinguished themselves as Protestant Catholics and Roman Catholics. William Penn once wrote, "I am a Catholic, but not a Roman Catholic."

On the first of September in this year, Captain

---

[1] Davis in "Day-star of Freedom."

James Neale,[1] an experienced mariner, who had lived in Spain, now settled on a large estate near the mouth of the Wicomico River, not far from St. Mary, and a prominent citizen, arrived at Boston with two pinnaces, commissioned by Governor Calvert to buy mares and sheep; but having bills of exchange on Lord Baltimore, in England, which could not be negotiated, owing to the civil war then raging, he was unsuccessful. While there, one of his pinnaces was discovered to be so worm-eaten that it was necessary to abandon it near the coast, where the May Flower had first landed her passengers, and perhaps the little ship was the "Dove" that had been to Boston once, and eight years before brought the first settlers to St. Mary.

A few weeks later, another coasting vessel from Virginia arrived at Boston with a Mr. Bennett, bearing a letter written at Nansemond or Upper Norfolk, on May the twenty-fourth, and signed by Richard Bennett, Daniel Gooking, John Hill, and seventy-one others, earnestly asking for faithful ministers. American Congregational-

---

[1] One of the Councillors of Maryland, and the ancestor of Archbishop Neale, the successor of Carroll

In 1666, he petitions the Assembly for the naturalization of his four children, "Henrietta, Maria, James, Dorothy, and Anthony Neale, born in Spain, of Ann his wife, during his residence there as a merchant, and when employed there by the King and Duke of York in several emergent affairs."—*Bacon's Laws of Maryland.*

ism found its earliest though brief home in Virginia.

In the very first ships that came to the mouth of the James River, were Puritan families, and they wrote back inviting their friends to follow; but Bishop Bancroft "being informed that great numbers were preparing to embark, obtained a proclamation prohibiting them to transport themselves to Virginia without a special license from the King."

Governor Wyatt stated, in 1623, that there were ministers in the colony, but not in orders;[1] and the next year there came to Virginia the learned and devout Puritan divine Henry Jacob, the first Congregational minister in England. He was born in Kent, educated at St. Mary's Hall, where he took the degree of A. M., entered into holy orders, and became precentor of Christ Church College, and afterward preached at Cheriton.[2]

---

[1] Cal. State Papers, Col. Series.

[2] Wood says he entered college at fifteen, and was "excellently well read." He published several works, the titles of which were:

Treatise on the Sufferings and Victory of Christ in the work of our Redemption, written against certain errors in these parts, publicly preached in London. London, 1598, 4to.

Treatise to show that the Church of England was a true Church. 1599.

Defence of the Treatise on Redemption, etc. 1600.

Reasons for reforming our Churches. 1604.

In 1599 he wrote a treatise to show that the Church of England was a true church, but visiting Leyden, he became acquainted with Robinson, and adopted the views of the Congregationalists, and returning, established the first Independent Church in England, and continued its pastor till, desirous of being more useful, he left his flock and departed for the wilderness of Virginia, where he soon died.

Daniel Gookins,[1] one of the best and bravest

A Position against vain-glorious and that which is falsely called learned preaching. 1604.

Plain and clear Exposition of Second Commandment. 1610.

His son Henry became a critical scholar, and assisted the learned Selden in his Hebrew studies.

[1] Daniel Gookins was one of the best men of his day, prominently identified with Virginia, Maryland, and Massachusetts.

He was a native of Kent, England, but came with his father, whose name was also Daniel, from Ireland to Virginia. The father arrived on the 22d of November, 1621, "with fifty men of his own, and thirty passengers, exceedingly well furnished with all sorts of provisions and cattle," and settled at Newport News.

When the Indians attacked the colonists, the old records say that he did not comply with the order, to retreat to a central blockhouse. "Master Gookins, having thirty-five of all sorts with him, made good his point against the savages."

Gov. Wyatt, on April 7th, 1623, writes to John Ferrar: "A ship has lately arrived, with forty men and thirty passengers, for Mr. Gookins."

There is an indenture on record, dated Feb. 1st, 1630, between Daniel Gookins, Gent., and Thos. Addison, his servant. In 1637 he obtained a grant of 2500 acres upon the northwest of Nansemond River. In 1642 he was President of the Court

men the New World had received, was then the owner of a plantation at Newport News, and at

---

of Upper Norfolk, and was then thirty years of age, and about that time made the acquaintance of Tompson. He owned a plantation near South River, Maryland, although after 1644 he became a resident of Massachusetts, yet keeping up business relations with the settlers on the Chesapeake. In 1655 two Indians murdered two of his negro servants, near South River. Says Davis: "Mary, the servant who had escaped, notwithstanding the severity of her wound, was the chief witness. But Warcosse, the Emperor, had sent down to St. Mary's some articles found in possession of the suspected Indians, and which it was known had belonged to Captain Gookins. And the Indians, who spoke through interpreters, confessed at the trial they were present at the murder—at one moment admitting, at the next denying, their guilt, 'fearful and desiring,' says the record, 'to conceal it.' They were convicted, sentenced, and executed on the same day." Gookins was a warm friend of John Eliot, the apostle to the New England Indians, and wrote a history of these Indians, and also of New England. Chief Justice Sewall called to see him when dying, and in his journal of that day records the fact of visiting, and expressively adds, "a right good man." His tombstone is still seen at Cambridge, Mass., with this inscription:

HERE LYETH INTERRED
YE BODY OF
MAJOR-GENERAL DANIEL GOOKINS,
AGED 75 YEARES,
WHO DEPARTED THIS LIFE
YE 19TH MARCH, 1686-7.

Gov. Gookins, of Pennsylvania, was a cousin, described by Wm. Penn in these words: "He is sober, understands to command and obey, moderate in his temper, and of what they call a good family: his grandfather, Sir Vincent Gookins, having

Nansemond, on the opposite bank of the James. The petition of the Virginia Congregationalists was read at a public lecture, and the ministers of Boston and vicinity set apart a day for its consideration, after which they selected three of their best men to respond to the call of Gookins and others for ministers. After some changes and delays, John Knowles, a ripe scholar from Immanuel College, and who had been pastor at Watertown; Thomas James, for ten years a faithful preacher at Charlestown; and William Tompson,[1] educated at Oxford University, started forth on the errand of love. After being wrecked at Hell Gate, in Long Island Sound, and exposed to the storms of winter, they reached Virginia in eleven weeks from the time of their departure. Men of the greatest personal dignity, and bearing letters from the Governor of Massachusetts, they were coldly received by Berkeley, the Governor of Virginia, and his chaplain, the Rev. Thomas Harrison. Unacknowledged by the authorities, they were greeted by well-disposed persons. Winthrop says: "Though the State did

---

been an early great planter in Ireland, in King James the First and Charles's days."

The entire letter of Penn may be found in Proud's Hist. of Pa., vol. ii. pp. 4 and 5.

[1] William Tompson, as the name was usually written, was born in Lancashire, Eng., in 1598, and graduated at Oxford in 1619. Before emigrating to America, he preached at Winwick. He died Dec. 10th, 1666.

silence the ministers, because they would not conform to the order of England, yet the people resorted to them in private houses to hear them as before."

After five or six months, Knowles and James seem to have returned to Massachusetts Colony, while Tompson, accompanied by Gookins and others, emigrated to Maryland, in the neighborhood of South and Severn Rivers, near the site of Annapolis. They were not looked upon as intruders, but welcomed as most desirable, and more of the same sort invited. Governor Winthrop, in his journal, under date of eighth month, thirteenth day, 1643, O. S., wrote: "The Lord Baltimore being the owner of much land near Virginia, being himself a Papist, and his brother, Mr. Calvert, the Governor there, a Papist also, but the colony consisting of both Papists and Protestants, he wrote a letter to Captain Gibbons, of Boston, and sent him a commission, wherein he made a tender of land in Maryland to any of ours that would transport themselves thither, with free liberty of religion, and all other privileges which the place affords."

The Indians of Virginia, like the Sioux of Minnesota during our late troubles, learning that the whites in England were engaged in war with each other, on April the eighteenth, 1644, a black Good Friday in the colonial calendar, suddenly swarmed around the feeble settlements in the valley of the James River, and as quickly disappeared, with their hands full of reeking scalps. Strong men fainted with horror; women moaned and refused to be comforted, for their children were not; the rich and the poor, the high and the low, overwhelmed by the common calamity, felt that it was a judgment of God for their sinfulness.[1]

Among those who were changed men was Thomas Harrison, the Governor's chaplain. He had been a bigot before, and though he kept a fair exterior to the godly men from Massachusetts, he now confessed that he had privately used his influence to have them silenced. But after the massacre, stung with remorse, he preached faithfully, which Berkeley thought was Puritanical, and he dismissed him, because he did not need so grave a chaplain.

Not cast down, he sought out the scattered flock of Nansemond, that remained after Tompson and others had left, and ministered unto their wants.

---

[1] The following law forcibly exhibits the feeling of the colony at this time:

"Enacted by the Governor, Council, and Burgesses of this Grand Assembly, for the public benefit of the colony, to the end that God mayeth avert his heavy judgments that are upon us, that the last Wednesday in every month be set apart for fasting and humiliation, and that it be wholly dedicated to prayers and preaching."

On the ninth of June, 1647, Leonard Calvert, the first Governor of the Maryland Colony, died, and Mistress Margaret Brent, an unmarried person, was left his administratrix. With truly Elizabethan vigor, she discharged her trust, and demanded a vote in the Provincial Assembly, which being denied, she protested against their acts. John Lewger, the first Secretary of the province, having buried his wife, soon returned to England, became a Roman Catholic priest, and lived in Lord Baltimore's house.

The Rev. William Tompson, described as one of "tall and comely presence," lost his wife a few months after he left Massachusetts, but he labored on in the colony until the latter part of 1648, winning golden opinions by his quiet, conservative, and Christian course. Mather, in a commemorative poem, says:

> "Hearers, like doves, flocked with contentious wing
> Who should be first, feed most, most homeward bring
> Laden with honey, like Hyblœan bees,
> They knead it into combs, upon their knees.
> * * * * * * *
> A constellation of great converts there
> Shone round him, and his heavenly glory wear,
> Gookins was one of them, by Tompson's pains,
> Christ and New England, a dear Gookins gains."

Some one visiting England about the close of the year 1647, perhaps John Lewger, tried to poison the mind of Lord Baltimore against Tompson. The Provincial Assembly of the next year thus earnestly resents the whisperings of the slanderer: "Whereas your Lordship doth seem to be greatly distasted and disgusted at William Tompson, your Lordship's old servant, through some information which has been given your Lordship of his comportment here, in aiding and siding with the rebels against your Lordship's governor and government, which information we do assure your Lordship to be a most false proceeding, rather, as we may suppose, out of hatred and spleen toward him, than any good affection or love toward your Lordship, for before anything was proceeded on in the Assembly William Tompson was called and strictly examined before the Governor, and Council, and whole Assembly, and nothing at all could be proved against him, wherewith he was accused to your Lordship, that was in that point most innocent; and further report of him, that your honor *hath not a more faithful and cordial friend* in the whole province, and shown to the utmost of his ability even before, in time of, and ever since the troubles here, than William Tompson is. Therefore we humbly crave of your honor, according to your honor's wonted clemency, not to harbor such thoughts, and give ear to such false suggestions against him; and further, my Lord seeing it hath been so notorious an injury and infamy to him, we humbly crave that your Lordship will intimate hither the next year who were his principal accusers on this point, which we the more earnestly beg, for that it will give the whole country and himself great satisfaction."

Tompson was a delicate and sensitive man, and though he could not but have been flattered, by the testimony of the colonial assembly, he soon left, and returned to preach and to die amid his old parishioners in Braintree, near Boston.

About this time, while the General Court was in session, the Rev. Mr. Harrison, of Virginia, visited Boston, in company with Durand, one of his elders, and stated that his church numbered one hundred and eighteen communicants, and that several of the council and nearly a thousand persons sympathized with their mode of worship, but owing to the Governor's hostility they would be obliged to seek a new home; Lord Baltimore had appointed at this time William Stone, a Protestant, formerly sheriff of Northampton County, Virginia, governor of his colony, and the members of Harrison's church were invited to settle near Annapolis. Harrison did not remain with them long, but returned to England, and reported the arbitrary conduct of Govenor Berkeley. On October the eleventh, 1649, the Council of State wrote to the Governor that they had been informed, by petition of the congregation of Nansemond, in Virginia, that their minister, Mr. Harrison, an able man, of unblamable conversation, had been banished the colony because he would not conform to the use of the Common Prayer Book. "As the Governor cannot be ignorant that the use of it is prohibited by Parliament, he is directed to permit Mr. Harrison to return to his ministry, unless there is sufficient cause approved by Parliament."

Although at first Cecil Baltimore adhered to King Charles, yet as the Parliament forces, under an old Yorkshire friend, Sir Thomas Fairfax, began to conquer, he veered to the side of the people, and to obviate any objections that might be offered not only appointed William Stone, a Protestant, governor of the colony, but also sent out to the Assembly a carefully prepared law to be passed, styled "An Act concerning Religion," embodying the distinctive features of recent Puritan legislation concerning the Sabbath, a wide contrast to the permission for dancing, vaulting, and archery, and other sports which had been allowed on Sunday, by King Charles.

It provided "That every person or persons within this province that shall at any time hereafter profane the Sabbath, or Lord's day, called Sunday, by frequent swearing, drunkenness, or by any uncivil or disorderly recreation, or by working on that day when absolute necessity doth not require," shall be fined. But in case the offenders should not have the ability to pay the fine imposed, it was provided that the persons should be imprisoned till they were ready to make open confession, and for the third offense they were to be publicly whipped.

It further declared, that any one that should deny the Holy Trinity should be punished with death and confiscation of goods.

It also prohibited the use of any reproachful words concerning "the blessed Virgin Mary, the mother of our Saviour, or the holy Apostles or Evangelists, and the calling of any one in a reproachful way heretic, schismatic, idolater, Puritan, Presbyterian, Independent, Popish Priest, Jesuit, Jesuited Papist, Lutheran, Anabaptist, Brownist, Antinomian, Barrowist, Roundhead, and Separatist, or any other name."

The Assembly of 1649, to which Lord Baltimore's law was submitted, consisted of the Governor, a Protestant, six councillors, and nine burgesses; and those who have carefully examined the early records feel confident that five of the burgesses were Roman Catholics, and three of the councillors.[1]

The law remitted to them was much more minute than any that had been before presented, and the oath of fidelity to the Proprietor was a recent requirement, and while they could not well do otherwise than pass the act that was sub-

---

[1] Davis.

mitted, they took occasion to write to the Proprietary these words:

"We do further humbly request your Lordship that hereafter such things as your Lordship may desire of us, may be done with as little swearing as conveniently may be, experience teaching us that a great occasion is given to much perjury when swearing becometh common. Forfeitures, perhaps, will be more efficacious to keep men honest, than swearing. Oaths little prevail upon men of little conscience. And, lastly, we do humbly request your Lordship hereafter to send us no more such bodies of laws, which serve to little other end than to fill our heads with suspicions, jealousies, and dislikes of that which verily we understand not; rather we shall desire your Lordship to send some short heads of what is desired, and then we do assure your Lordship of a most forward willingness in us to give your Governor all just satisfaction that can be thought reasonable."

Edward Gibbons, once a gay young man, then a person of weight around Boston, and their chief military officer, had for years traded with the Maryland Colony, and while in England became acquainted with Lord Baltimore. It was therefore wise policy, now that Charles was beheaded, and the battles of Naseby and Marston Moor had proved that there was truth, as well as sarcasm, in the song of the Cavalier,

"Although they snuffled psalms, to give
These rebel dogs their due,
When the roaring shot poured thick and hot,
They were stalwart men and true,"

to conciliate Parliament and its friends in his colony, and he tendered to Gibbons, in 1650, a commission as Admiral of the province and councillor. While the records show that Gibbons owned a windmill at Saint Mary, he does not appear to have become a permanent resident of the colony.

The Assembly of 1650, it is admitted by all, had a Protestant majority,[1] and they created an upper and lower house, to meet apart, the Governor and council constituting the upper, a form of government which remained unchanged until the American revolution. They also struck out from the oath of fidelity, prescribed by Lord Baltimore, the expressions of "absolute Lord"

---

[1] Members of Assembly, 1650:

Saint Mary's County.

St. George Hundred—John Hatch, P.; Walter Beane, P.

Newtown Hundred—John Medley; Wm. Brough, P.; Robert Robins, P.

St. Clements Hundred—Francis Posey, P.

St. Mary's Hundred—Philip Land; Francis Brooks.

St. Inigos Hundred—Cuthbert Fenwick.

St. Michael's Hundred--Thos. Sterman, P.; George Manners.

Providence or Ann Arundel County.

James Cox, P.; George Puddington, P.

Those marked P were Protestants.

and "royal jurisdiction," and inserted that they would defend all his lordship's rights "not any wise understood to infringe or prejudice liberty of conscience and religion." The settlements of Providence were also this year organized into a county, named after the recently deceased wife of the Proprietary, Ann Arundel.[1]

Charles the Second, an exile at Breda, hearing of Baltimore's turning to the Parliament, commissioned Sir William Davenant, the god-son of Shakspeare, as Governor of Maryland, "alleging therein the reason to be because Lord Baltimore did visibly adhere to the rebels in England, and admitted all kinds of sectaries and schismatics and ill-affected persons into that plantation."

With the aid of Queen Henrietta Maria, Davenant collected a company of French mechanics and weavers, and sailed from a port in Normandy for America; but on the sea he was captured by a Parliament ship, brought to England, and lodged in the Tower, where he finished his poem of Gondibert, and was at length released from

---

[1] Ann Arundel, the wife of Cecil, Lord Baltimore, and daughter of Thomas Arundel, Baron of Wardour, died on the 23d of July, 1649, in the 34th year of her age. The following is one of the inscriptions on her tomb at Tisbury:

"Anna Arundelia, pulcherrima et optima conjux Cecilii Calverti Baronis de Baltemore, et absolu: domini Terræ Mariæ, et Avaloniæ, Filiaq: Charissima Thomæ Arundeliæ, Primi Baronis de Warder et sac Romp. Imp. Comitis."

"durance vile" by the intercession of the great Puritan poet, John Milton.

In concluding this article on the formative period of the colony, it will not be inappropriate to glance at the subsequent career of those who had been the pioneer religious teachers among the early settlers of Maryland. Father Andrew White returned to England and died on December the twenty-seventh, 1656.

John Lewger having become a Roman Catholic priest,[1] and inmate of Lord Baltimore's house, plunged into the theological controversies of the hour, and in 1659 published a work entitled "Erastus Junior, a solid demonstration by principles, forms of ordination, common laws, acts of Parliament, that no Bishop nor Presbyter hath any authority to preach from Christ, but from Parliament." This, three years later, was followed by "Erastus Senior, scholastically demonstrating the conclusion that admitted Lambeth Records to be true, those called Bishops here in

---

[1] Benjamin Denham, Chaplain of Earl of Winchester, on Jan. 27, 1667, writes from Pera, near Constantinople:

"Surprised at the appointment of Marquis of Dorchester. All that is treated of in the Privy Council about Roman Catholics is discovered to Lord Brudenell and Lord Baltimore, Governor of Maryland, whose Chaplain, an English recusant, now a Romish priest, was one of the vicegerents there, in Charles the First's time."—*Cal. State Papers, Dom. Series.*

England, are no Bishops either in order or jurisdiction, or so much as legal."

When the plague raged in London, he exposed himself in visiting poor sick Roman Catholics, and died of that disease in 1665 at St. Giles-in-the-Fields.

The scholarly Knowles, on visiting his native land, found many of his schoolmates in prominent places, and his ability as a preacher, for a period, gave him Bristol Cathedral as a field of labor, but on the restoration of Charles the Second, he refused to conform, and was silenced.

After leaving Bristol, he preached for sixteen years at Pershore, in Worcester, and on April the ninth, 1665, his house was searched, goods seized, and himself imprisoned for sedition, because he had collected money for suffering Polanders, which in his petition for release, he quaintly says "he did not know was unlawful, but thought them an object of pity." On his release, he devoted himself to those suffering from the plague in London, and at the ripe age of fourscore and five years, on April the tenth, 1685, was gathered to his fathers.

Lord Baltimore, in 1651, in a letter to the Assembly of Maryland, alludes with respect to Dr. Thomas Harrison, who appears then to have been in London, and was for some time the minister of St. Dunstan's East.

When the upright Harry Cromwell, respected by foes, and loved by friends, became Viceroy of Ireland, he accompanied him as Chaplain, and was very useful as a preacher in Dublin. Several of his letters are printed in the Thurloe State Papers, and he published a work called "Topica Sacra," and in 1659 a sermon called "Threni Hibernici, or Ireland sympathizing with England and Scotland in a sad lamentation for the loss of her Josiah."

As he advanced in years, like Richard Baxter, he suffered from persecution, and in the Calendar of State Papers for 1665, there is a report dated Chester, July the third, of which the following is the substance: "A conventicle of one hundred persons was appointed at the house of Dr. Thomas Harrison, late Chaplain of Harry Cromwell; broke open the house, found some under the beds, others in the closets, and thirty were taken before the Mayor."

Refined, a fluent speaker, an earnest Christian, he was greatly admired, and the Earl of Thomond used to say "he had rather hear Dr. Harrison say grace over an egg, than hear the Bishops pray or preach."

In one of the Camden Society Publications[1]

---

[1] Smith's Obituaries.

is the last notice we have of Sir William Berkeley's chaplain:

"1665, Oct. 13. Dr. Thomas Harrison, preacher at St. Christopher's, and before at St. Bartholomew's, died ex peste. Was buried on the fourteenth."

CHAPTER THIRD.

DIFFICULTIES WITH VIRGINIANS, AND FROM CIVIL WAR IN ENGLAND.

SAMUEL MATTHEWS and William Clayborne were two of the Virginia Councillors who, in October, 1629, refused to allow Lord George Baltimore to settle in the colony, unless he complied with the law of England, and took the oath of allegiance and supremacy. Partly on this account their subsequent relations with his son and successor, Cecil Baltimore, were not very pleasant.

Matthews owned the best estate in the colony, on the River James, just above Newport News, and was thrifty and intelligent.[1] His wife was the daughter of Sir Thomas Hinton. His plantation was a miniature village; the flax and hemp were there made into fabrics; the cattle not only furnished beef for the ships bound for England, but the hides were tanned, and the leather made into shoes. The dairy was large,

[1] The early manuscript records of the Virginia Company, show that he received a patent as early as 1622.

and live stock of all kinds abundant. At his own cost, moreover, he began the erection of a fort at Point Comfort.

Loyal to the King, he esteemed it a part of his religion, before the days of the Commonwealth, to denounce Papists and Puritans.[1] He was a type of the early planter; "lived bravely, kept a good house, and was a true lover of Virginia."

Clayborne was also a representative man. He came to the colony in 1621, as Surveyor; soon became a Councillor; was for many years Secretary of State, and explored the Chesapeake; established a trading post at Palmer's Isle, at the mouth of the Susquehanna, and made a settlement at Kent Island, at least three years before the patent for Maryland was issued. He visited England shortly after George Baltimore's return, and on the sixteenth of May, 1631, was, with his associates, licensed to trade in those parts for which a patent had not already been granted. As soon as it was known that Lord Baltimore had comprehended the land already occupied within his patent, William Cloberry, John de la Barre, and David Moorhead, of London, partners of Clayborne, remonstrated, on the ground that they had already purchased the Isle of Kent, and began a settlement.

The planters of Virginia, when they heard of

---

[1] Hammond, in "Leah and Rachel."

the grant by the King to Baltimore, appealed to the Privy Council, and urged that he might be asked to settle in some other place. On the twenty-eighth of June, 1633, both sides were heard; and on the third of July, an order was issued from the Star Chamber, which was an evasion rather than a final decision, as it "left Lord Baltimore to his patent, and the other parties to the course of law according to their desires." The announcement of the action of the Privy Council of England in Virginia, created not only surprise, but a feeling of insecurity; and before Leonard Calvert and the Maryland colonists arrived, the Governor and Council of Virginia informed the home government "that, in consequence of a grant to Lord Baltimore, the inhabitants are importunate for a confirmation of their lands and privileges by the King."

After Leonard Calvert landed at Jamestown, and before the town of Saint Mary was purchased from the Indians, William Clayborne appeared at a meeting of the Virginia Council, and stated that Governor Calvert had told him that he was no longer a member of the Virginia Colony, but belonged to his plantation, and desired their advice as to the proper course for him to pursue.

"It was answered by the Board, that they wondered why such question was made; that they knew no reason why they should render up the right of the Isle of Kent, more than any other formerly given to this colony by his Majesty's patent; and that the right of my Lord's grant being yet undetermined in England, we are bound in duty and by our oaths to maintain the rights and privileges of the colony."

The Privy Council of England, on the twenty-second of July, 1634, also said that "it is not intended that interests which men have settled when you were a corporation should be impeached."

While the Councillors of Virginia sympathized with Clayborne, Sir John Harvey, appointed Governor by King Charles, was ready by every means in his power to sustain Cecil Baltimore and Governor Calvert; Windebank, Secretary of the Privy Council in England, was also a strong friend to Baltimore, being a Roman Catholic in his sympathies.

The complete understanding between these parties is proved by their correspondence. Cecil Baltimore, while at Warder Castle,[1] on September the fifteenth, sent his brother-in-law, William Peasley, to beg Windebank to procure a letter from the King to Sir John Harvey, thanking him for the assistance he had given to the Maryland plantation, against "Clayborne's malicious behavior." If such letter was not sent by the

---

[1] Warder Castle, the seat of Earl Arundel, his wife's father.

ship now ready to sail, he feared his plantation might be overthrown.

Windebank, not waiting for the King's letter, three days after this request, wrote a flattering letter to Harvey; and on the twenty-ninth it was followed by a note from the King. He stated that he had given the grant to Lord Baltimore, "there being land enough for the entertainment of many thousands, and the work more easily overcome by multitudes of hands and assistance," and he thanks Governor Harvey for his ready assistance to the plantation begun in Maryland, and requires him to continue the same.

But the sturdy freemen of Virginia could not be made to believe that the usurpation was lawful, although sanctioned by an arbitrary King. The people of Kent Isle had been represented by delegates in their Assembly,[1] and they did not wish these relations sundered. While Governor Harvey was elated by the notice of the King, through Baltimore's instigation, he was also humiliated by the little influence he had with the people of Virginia. The pliant and despotic tool of the Court, on December the sixteenth, despondingly wrote to Windebank:

"Is desirous to do Lord Baltimore all the service he is able, but his power is not great, being

---

[1] Hening's Statutes, vol. i.

limited by his commission to the greater number of voices at the Council table, where almost all are against him, especially when it concerns Maryland. Many are so averse to that plantation, that they proclaim and make it their familiar talk, that they would rather knock their cattle on the heads, than sell them to Maryland. He suspects the faction is nourished in England, and also by Capt. Sam. Matthews, who, scratching his head and in a fury stamping, cried out: 'a pox upon Maryland.' "

It was unfortunate for Leonard Calvert, upon his arrival at Saint Mary, to be associated with one so indiscreet as Harvey. If prudent measures had been at first taken, Clayborne might have become a valuable assistant; but harsh measures were at an early period initiated.

In the face of the order of the King,[1] dated October the eighth, 1634, requiring the planters of Kentish Island to be assisted, that they may enjoy the fruit of their labors, and forbidding Baltimore or his agents to do them violence, Governor Calvert acted as if the question as to

---

[1] The King wrote from Hampton Court, Oct. 8, 1634, to the Governor and Council of Virginia, and to all Lieutenants of Provinces in America:

"Requires them to be assisting the planters in Kentish Island, that they may peaceably enjoy the fruits of their labors, and forbids Lord Baltimore or his agents to do them any violence." —*State Paper Cal., Col. Series*, 1574–1660.

the right of the Kent Islanders had been fully determined. As had been their custom, some of these Islanders went, in the spring of 1635, to trade with the Indians on the Pocomoke River, in a pinnace called the Longtail, and on the twenty-third of April the boat and goods were seized by the Marylanders.

Clayborne, indignant at the hostile act, sent a boat from Virginia, in command of Ratcliffe Warren, to recover the goods and captured vessel. In the harbor of great Wiggomoco, Warren met Captain Cornwallis of St. Mary, in the pinnace St. Margaret, and on the tenth of May a fight occurred between the rival parties. Warren, with John Bellson and William Dawson, of the Virginia party, were killed, and Thomas Smith, Gent., taken prisoner, while the Marylanders lost but one man, William Ashmore.[1] The collision caused great excitement in both colonies. About the time of this occurrence, the arbitrary conduct of Harvey led to a revolution in Virginia. Capt. Sam. Matthews, on the twenty-eighth of April, with forty musketeers, surrounded his house, and John Utie, placing his

---

[1] At a meeting of the Privy Council of England, it was stated that "Lord Baltimore's servants had slain three men at the entrance of Hudson's River, which goes to Maryland."—*State Paper Cal , Col. Series.*

Hudson River is a broad arm of the bay between the Choptauk and Taylor's Island.

hand upon his shoulder, said, "I arrest you for treason." He was then told to prepare for England, where he must go and answer their complaints. Perfectly powerless in the face of a strong public sentiment, he submitted, and the colonists, with their strong republican tendencies, chose in his stead John West, brother of Lord Delawarr.

On the twenty-third of May, Clayborne was at Elizabeth City, and wrote to England that all his rights had been trampled upon, and the King's express commands, under the protection of which he deemed himself so safe, had been contemned, and he had perished by security.

Matthews, writing to Sir John Wostenholme, said that Clayborne had applied two days since for redress against the oppression of the Marylanders, who had slain three and hurt other inhabitants of the Isle of Kent, and he did not believe they would have committed such outrages without Harvey's instigation. He concludes "with an assured hope that Sir John Harvey's return [to England] will be acceptable to God, not displeasing to his Majesty, and an assured happiness unto this Colony." At White Hall, on December the eleventh, the Privy Council met to inquire into the causes of Harvey's being in England, and the King said that it was an assumption of the regal power upon the part of the colonists, and that Harvey should go back to

Virginia, "though to stay but a day." Cecil Baltimore, finding the King in this temper, requested the arrest of John West, Samuel Mattnews, and others, and that they might be brought to England to answer for their misdemeanors; also that the Attorney-General might draw out a new commission for Harvey, with enlarged powers, and that Secretary Windebank prepare his instructions.

Jerome Hawley, the associate councillor of Cornwallis, in Maryland, was now in England and preparing to go back with Harvey, having obtained, through Cecil Baltimore's court influence, the position of Treasurer as well as Councillor of the Colony of Virginia. The persistent Baltimore, on February the twenty-fifth, 1637, through his brother-in-law, Peasley, tells Windebank that he considered the proposition concerning the advancement of the King's service in Virginia, and is well assured of his own ability to perform with ample satisfaction what he undertakes, and proposes a way of moving the King in this business, which is most likely to take effect.

If the memorial was not on file, it would be difficult to believe that Baltimore proposed to increase the annual revenue from Virginia £8000, on condition that he was made Governor of that colony with a salary of £2000 per annum.[1]

---

[1] State Paper Cal., Col. Series, 1574–1660, p. 250.

Although Jerome Hawley had been appointed Treasurer and Councillor of Virginia before he left England,[1] he appeared at Saint Mary and sat as a member of the second assembly in that province, which commenced its sessions on the twenty-first day of January, 1637–8, and at the close of which Thomas Smith, Gent., of the Isle of Kent, an associate of Warren in the Pocomoke affair, was tried for piracy and felony, and condemned to be hung, and a bill of attainder passed against William Clayborne, by which his property was forfeited to the Lord Proprietor.

Before the Act was passed by the Maryland Assembly, Clayborne was in England refuting the charges against him, and complaining that Baltimore's agents, with forty men, had gone to take possession of his trading post on Palmer's Isle, at the mouth of the Susquehanna. He, at the same time, offered to pay yearly one hundred

---

[1] Jerome Hawley was in London on June 27, 1636, and wrote to Windebank that he would visit him on the next Sunday. In August, he sailed in the "Black George" with Sir John Harvey for Virginia, but owing to leakage the ship returned. In April, 1637, he sailed in the Friendship. Geo. Reade, of Jamestown, writing to his brother, a secretary of Windebank's, says: "Mr. Hawley has not proved the man he took him for, having neither given any satisfaction for money received of him nor brought him any servants."

He died in the summer of 1638, leaving a childless widow, and his associate councillor of the Maryland Colony, Thomas Cornwallis, was his administrator.

pounds sterling to the Crown for possession of the Isle of Kent and the Susquehanna plantation, with twelve leagues of land in that country.

The King approved the proposals, and ordered a day for a full hearing of the complaint. Cecil Baltimore was now alarmed, and writes to the King "that he is informed that upon a representation lately exhibited for renewing a Virginia Company their request was granted, although his Majesty said he would not have the petitioner's interest in Maryland anyways impeached, yet it is intended to infringe upon his government."

The unstable Charles, in every matter of importance, always oscillating when men wished him to stand firm, now writes to the Commissioners for foreign Plantations not to allow any patent or warrant for plantation or discovery near Avalon[1] and Maryland to pass the seals, which in any way may infringe upon the rights of Lord Baltimore, and engages his royal word never to permit any quo warranto or other pro-

---

[1] About the time of these promises Avalon was granted to other parties. Sir David Kirk writes from Ferryland, Oct. 2, 1639, to Archbishop Laud: "Out of one hundred persons they took over, only one died of sickness. The air of Newfoundland agrees perfectly well with all God's creatures, except Jesuits and schismatics. A great mortality amongst the former tribe so affrighted my Lord of Baltimore, that he utterly deserted the country."

ceedings for infringing or overthrowing either of his patents.

At length, on the fourth of April, 1638, the Commissioners of Plantations reported the right and title to the Isle of Kent to be absolutely with him, and that the violences complained of by Clayborne to be left to the ordinary course of justice.[1]

But, on July the fourteenth, 1638, the King from Greenwich writes to Cecil Baltimore:

"The King understands that contrary to his pleasure, Lord Baltimore's agents have slain three persons, possessed themselves of the island by force, and seized the persons and estates of the planters. These disorders have been referred to the Commissioners for Plantations. He is therefore commanded to allow the planters and their agents to have free enjoyment of their possessions without further trouble, until the cause is decided."[2]

Clayborne, on the eighth of August, 1640, appointed George Serrell, of Nansemond, Virginia, to collect any debts due him in Maryland, but the Governor and Council, to the petition of Ser-

---

[1] Wm. Penn searched the records for an authenticated copy of this report, but it could never be found. Lord Charles Baltimore also failed in his search.

[2] State Paper Cal., Col. Series, p. 280.

rell, presented a tart and laconic reply, stating that all the property of Clayborne had been forfeited for piracy and murder.

Sir John Harvey on his return to Virginia, with his secretary, Richard Kemp, who, in 1638, built the first brick mansion, "the fairest ever known in this country for substance and uniformity," were more despotic than before in their sway. He who dared differ from them in opinion quickly felt the weight of their displeasure. Kemp having some difficulty with the Rev. Anthony Panton, rector of York and Cheskiack, banished him from the colony in 1639, for alleged "mutinous, rebellious, and riotous acts." The minister was not a man tamely to submit to injustice, and his report of Kemp's conduct excited high displeasure in England. As Kemp had always befriended Cecil Baltimore, he writes to him on August the twentieth, 1640, and begs his interest with the Archbishop of Canterbury that he may be satisfied with his conduct, and preserved against injury and malice; but the influence asked seems to have availed nothing, for on October the thirtieth, 1641, upon petition of Anthony Panton, Clerk and Minister in Virginia, and Agent for the Church and Clergy there, it was ordered by the House of Lords, "that Sir W. Berkeley, Kt., Richard Kemp, and Christopher Wormsley, shall be stayed their voyage, and forthwith answer the complaint in the said petition."[1]

In the year 1642 hostilities commenced between the Royalist and Parliament forces in England, and at first both Lord Baltimore and Clayborne were on the side of the King. In March Baltimore's wife's brother, William Arundel, preferred charges against him, partly of a civil and partly of a criminal nature, and the House of Lords ordered him to give bonds not to leave the kingdom without permission, and the next month his old opponent, Clayborne, received a commission from Charles, as Treasurer of Virginia for life.

It became necessary now to be careful that he did not offend Parliament by transcending the letter of the Maryland charter, which, while it gave him the patronage of all churches, and the power to license the erection of chapels, also expressly provided that the same should "be dedicated and consecrated according to the ecclesiastical laws of England."

As early as 1635 it had been charged before the Privy Council that mass was celebrated in Maryland, and the Jesuits had boasted that they had made proselytes of nearly all the emigrants

---

[1] Neither Anderson in his "Colonial Churches," nor Bishop Meade in his "Old Parishes of Virginia," makes any mention of this Agent for the Church and Clergy of Virginia.

that arrived in the year sixteen hundred and thirty-eight.

Baltimore being anxious to preserve his Maryland possession, it is very easy to see why the chapel of Saint Mary should have been purchased in his name for £200,[1] and why he should have at that period disapproved of sending a reinforcement of Jesuits.

Politic, and looking for his own aggrandizement, he wrote on October the seventh, 1642: "Considering the dependence of the state of Maryland on the state of England, unto which it must, as near as may be, be conformable, no ecclesiastic in the province ought to expect, nor is Lord Baltimore, nor any of his officers, although they are Roman Catholics, obliged in conscience to allow to such ecclesiastics any more or other privileges, exemptions, or immunities for the persons, lands, or goods, than is allowed by his Majesty or officers to like persons in England."

In view of the increasing troubles of the king-

---

1 Speaking of this purchase, Baltimore, in a dispatch dated Bristol, July the fourteenth, 1643, tells Dep. Gov. Brent: "Owing to some mistakes in that business, I have thought fit not to accept" the bills drawn on him. On November the fourteenth, he speaks of sending Mr. Gilmett as an agent, and desires all his carpenters and other apprentice servants to be sold forthwith, and that the best endeavors be used to discharge the bargain for Mr. Copley's house at Saint Mary's. He does not call Father Copley's house the chapel at Saint Mary's, but it was probably the same.

dom, Governor Calvert left Maryland in April, 1643, to visit and consult his brother, Lord Baltimore. King Charles, a refugee at Oxford, that year granted commissions to Lord Baltimore, to surprise the Parliament and London ships, and also appointed Leonard Calvert to treat with the Assembly of Virginia relative to the exportation of tobacco and the transportation of goods; and appointed Lord Baltimore collector and receiver of all customs, with power to appoint deputies.

About the first of November, 1643, a ship left London for Maryland, commanded by Richard Ingle. Upon its arrival at Saint Mary, by virtue of the commission granted to Leonard Calvert by Charles the First to seize London ships commissioned by Parliament, acting Governor Brent captured the vessel, Ingle however escaping, and tendered the crew an oath against Parliament, and tampered with them to carry the ship to Bristol, that city being on the side of the King.

He also issued, on the twentieth of January, 1643–4, the following

"Proclamation against Richard Ingle.

"I do hereby require, in his Majesty's name, Richard Ingle, mariner, to yield his body to Robert Ellyson, sheriff of this county, before the first day of February next, to answer such crimes of treason as on his Majesty's behalf shall be objected against him, upon his utmost peril of the law in that behalf; and I do further require all persons that can say or disclose any matter of treason against the said Richard Ingle, to inform his Lordship's attorney of it at some time before the said court, to the end it may be then and there prosecuted."[1]

After an absence of eighteen months, Leonard Calvert returned in September, 1644, to resume his duties as Governor, and found not only the colony divided into factions by the civil war in the mother country, but also that Clayborne was once more asserting his claim to Kent Island.

Ingle, after his escape, returned to England in one of the vessels constantly sailing from Jamestown. He there obtained a letter of marque, and as captain of the ship Reformation, he departed again for Maryland—to use the words of his petition to the House of Lords—"where, finding the Governor of that province to have received a commission from Oxford to seize upon all ships belonging to London, and to execute a tyrannical power against the Protestants,

---

[1] De Vries, the celebrated Dutch mariner, passed most of the winter of 1643–4 at Sir W. Berkeley's, in Jamestown, Virginia. On April the thirteenth, 1644, on his way to Europe, he witnessed, at the mouth of Warwick Creek, near Newport News, a fight between a twelve-gun ship of Bristolers, as the Royalists were called, and two vessels of Londoners. Five days after this, on Good Friday, the Indians rose and massacred the inhabitants, to which allusion has been made in the last chapter.

and such as adhered to Parliament, and to press wicked oaths upon them, and endeavor their extirpation, he did venture his life and fortune in sending his men, and assisting the well affected Protestants against the tyrannical government, and it pleased God to enable him to take divers places from them." His success was so complete, and the people so fully in sympathy, that Leonard Calvert, Secretary Lewger, and their few adherents, fled to Virginia, and Captain Edward Hill was made Governor.[1]

On the twenty-fifth of December, 1645, there was read in the House of Lords the following paper, from the Committee of Plantations:

"DIE VENERIS, 28th Nov., 1645.

"The petition of divers in Maryland was this day read, setting forth the tyrannical government of that province ever since its first settling by recusants, who have reduced and forced many of his Majesty's subjects from their religion, and humbly praying the assistance and the

---

[1] The Virginia Assembly of 1645–6 passed the following:

"Whereas, Lieutenant Nicholas Stillwell, and others of the colony, have secretly conveyed themselves to Maryland, or Kent, and divers others engaged persons likely to follow, if timely prevention be not had therein;

"Be it therefore enacted, that Capt. Thos. Willoughby and Capt. Edward Hill be hereby authorized to go to Maryland, or Kent, to demand the return of such persons who are already departed from the colony."—*Hening's Statutes.*

protection of the Parliament, by appointing such a government as they shall think fit.

"Upon consideration whereof, as also the letters patent whereby his Majesty, in the eighth year of his reign, granted the said province to Cecil Calvert, Baron of Baltimore, and of a certificate from the Judge of the Admiralty, grounded upon the deposition of witnesses taken in that Court: That Leonard Calvert, late Governor there, had a commission from Oxford to seize such persons, ships, and goods as belonged to any of London; which he registered, proclaimed, and endeavored to put in execution at Virginia; and that one Brent, his deputy Governor, had seized upon a ship, empowered under a commission derived from the Parliament, because she was of London, and afterward not only tampered with the crew thereof to carry her to Bristol, then in hostility against the Parliament, but also tendered them an oath against the Parliament.

"This Committee doth therefore conceive that not only the said Governor and deputy Governor are unfit to be longer continued in the said charge, but also that the Lord Baltimore hath broken the trust reposed in them by said letters patent; and that it will be a very good service to have the said plantation and government settled in Protestants' hands by order of Parliament," etc.

During the year 1646, Cecil Baltimore was urging before the House of Lords a petition in behalf of his patent, but not with much success, and apparently fearing that it would be revoked, he wrote from Stook on the fifteenth of November, 1646, and gave a power of attorney to his brother, Leonard Calvert, and his trusty and well-beloved John Lewger, to collect all rents and dues belonging to him, either in Virginia or Maryland, and to dispose thereof as he should direct.

Clayborne now was in possession of Kent Island, and Ingle appears to have taken to England Father White and one or two other Jesuits, and the records he had captured.[1] Taking advantage of his absence, Leonard Calvert came back, with a small force, and regained possession of the government, and in April, 1647, he went in person and reduced Kent Island to his authority, and made Robert Vaughan, a Protestant, commander thereof. After a few months his health failed, and on the ninth of June he died, having on his sick bed appointed Mistress Margaret Brent, a single woman, his administra-

---

[1] Lord Baltimore ordered a special warrant to James Linsey and Richard Willam, for grant of the manor of Snow Hill, for services against Ingle, to be inserted in the patent, "a notice of their singular and approved worth, courage, and fidelity, to the end in memory of their merit."—*Kilty's Landholder's Assistant.*

trix,[1] and Thomas Green his successor, the same man who, on November the fifteenth, 1649, proclaimed the Prince of Wales "as the undoubted

---

[1] On November 22d, 1638, Giles, and Fulk, and Margaret, and Mary Brent arrived in the colony.

The Assembly recognized Miss Brent as the Attorney of the Lord Proprietary, and she then asked for a vote in that body for herself, and also as Attorney of Leonard Calvert. Governor Green refused, and she then protested against all the acts of the Assembly. Baltimore seems to have disapproved of Mistress Brent's course, but the Assembly of 1649 right gallantly defended her. They wrote:

"As for Mistress Brent's undertaking and meddling with your estate, we do verily believe, and in conscience report, that it was better for the colony's safety at that time in her hands, than in any man's else in the whole province after your brother's death; for the soldiers would never have treated any other with that civility and respect, and though they were even ready at several times to run into mutiny, yet she still pacified them, till at last things were brought to that strait, that she must be admitted and declared your Lordship's attorney by order of court, or else all must go to ruin again, and the second mischief had been doubtless far greater than the former; so that, if there hath not been any sinister use made of your Lordship's estate by her, from what it was intended and engaged for by Mr. Calvert before his death, as we verily believe she hath not; then we conceive from that time she rather deserved favor and thanks from your Honor, for her so much concurring to the public safety, than to be justly liable to all those bitter invectives you have been pleased to express against her."

Dep. Gov. Giles Brent moved across the river into Virginia at an early day. He had a son named Giles, and a grandson William, who were Virginians.

The latter died in England in 1709, at the age of twenty-five.

rightful heir to all his father's dominions," and as King Charles the Second.

The course of Ingle was approved in London, for, soon after this, he was recommended to be a commander of one of the Parliament ships.

After the visit of Leonard Calvert to his brother, reverse after reverse was the lot of the Royalists. On the fields of Marston Moor and Naseby, Sir Thomas Fairfax, with his Lieutenant Cromwell, had taught Rupert and the Cavaliers that the forces of Parliament could fight as well as pray, and those that used to laugh now began to tremble before the Roundheads. Royal pride and popular impatience wrestled together, until at last the latter forced the head of the King to the block, and the Parliament became the keeper of the liberties of England, and succeeded to all his rights.

To this revolution, self-interest prompted many of the courtiers to accede, and among them was Cecil Baltimore, who encouraged the Assembly of Maryland to imitate Parliament in passing laws against blasphemy, and assented to the expunging of the words "absolute Lord" and "royal jurisdiction" from the oath of fidelity to the Lord Proprietary.

Although Richard Ingle had been excepted in the Act of Oblivion by the Maryland Assembly, he was not inconvenienced thereby, for on March the first, 1650, before the Committee of

Admiralty, he preferred charges against Lord Baltimore concerning misdemeanors in his government of Maryland, and two weeks later, after several debates in the Committee "of the business depending between Captain Ingle and Lord Baltimore, touching a commission granted to Leonard Calvert, brother to the said Lord Baltimore, by the late King at Oxford, in 1643, the Attorney General and Dr. Walker were desired to take into consideration the validity and invalidity of the original grant of June twentieth, 1632, to Cecil Lord Baltimore of a tract of land called Maryland, and all parties interested were summoned to appear before them on the thirteenth of the month."

Baltimore from week to week delayed noticing the summons, and on the fifth of April they issued another order, requiring him to appear on the eighteenth, and that, if he did not, they would proceed to make a report.

No record has been found as to the final determination of the matter between Ingle and Baltimore, but on October the third the Council of State considered the petition and papers presented by Henry Wallis, in behalf of divers well-affected persons of the "Isle of Providence, in Maryland," and they declared that as Parliament had already expressed themselves sensible of the condition of the plantation depending upon the Commonwealth, and lately ordered the bringing in of the patents of the pretended proprietor, that the Council may proceed to take care of those plantations, but that for the present the matters of remonstrance by Mr. Wallis should be referred to a sub-committee.

In the hope of increasing the confidence of Parliament, and conciliating the republicans of Maryland, Lord Baltimore issued a commission, to which allusion has been made, for Edward Gibbons, Esq., Major-General of New England, to be councillor, justice of the peace, and admiral of the Province of Maryland. When the colonists heard of the discussions that had taken place in the Council of State and before the Admiralty Committee, it was not strange that they should have thought that the proprietary government would soon be dissolved. Edward Lloyd, Commander of Anne Arundel County, appears to have taken some step looking to a change of government, which, in a dispatch of Baltimore to the Assembly, dated August the twentieth, 1651, is thus noticed:

"We cannot but much wonder at a message, which we understood was lately sent by one Mr. Lloyd, from some lately seated at Anne Arundel, to our General Assembly, held at Saint Mary's, in March last, but are unwilling to impute, either to the sender or deliverer thereof, so malign a sense of ingratitude and other ill affections as it may seem to bear; conceiving rather that it proceeded from some apprehensions in them, at that time grounded upon some reports in those parts, of a dissolution or resignation here of our patent and right to that province." He then added, that they would learn, from Mr. Harrison[1] and other of their friends in England, that these reports were false.

A month after this was penned, Parliament appointed Captain Robert Dennis, Richard Bennett, Thomas Stagg, of Westover, and Captain William Clayborne, Commissioners to reduce the people in "all the plantations within the Bay of Chesapeake." Owing to the loss at sea of Captain Dennis and the frigate John, Captain Edward Curtis, in command of the Guinea frigate of twenty-eight guns, acted in connection with Clayborne and Bennett.

The Council of State, in addition to the instructions to the Commissioners, on October the second also prepared a letter for "Richard Bennet, Esq., in Virginia," with some instructions, which he was not to open until the country was obedient to the Commonwealth.

On the twelfth of March, 1652–3, the Governor and Council of Virginia surrendered to the Commissioners upon the most liberal terms. Neither

---

[1] Rev. Dr. Thomas Harrison, who had formed the Congregational Church of Nansemond, Virginia, a portion of whose members had moved to Severn River and vicinity in 1648–9.

the Governor nor Council were obliged to take any oath to the Commonwealth for one year, and were allowed passes to leave Virginia within a year, and to be free from arrest or trouble for six months after their arrival in England. The best men of the colony were opposed to Berkeley and the despotic officers of the Crown. Among others Colonel Richard Lee,[1] the ancestor of the Richard Lee, who in the Continental Congress offered the resolution declaring the colonies free and independent states.

Visiting Saint Mary, Governor Stone and Council were told that they did not intend to infringe Lord Baltimore's just rights, and they only desired conformity to the laws of the Commonwealth of England. They refused to conform, on the ground that it was inconsistent with the charter of the colony, and the oaths they had taken to Lord Baltimore. The Commissioners therefore proceeded, on the twenty-ninth of March, 1652, to establish a pro-

[1] In 1654 Colonel Richard Lee visited England, and brought some old silver to be melted over. In September, 1655, under the act forbidding the exportation of plate and bullion, his trunk, containing two hundred ounces of silver, in the new style, with his coat of arms engraved thereon, was seized at Gravesend, on board the ship Anthony. Upon petition of his London agent it was restored, "Colonel Lee being faithful and useful to the interest of the Commonwealth."—*Cal. State Papers, Col. Series*, 1574–1660, p. 430.

vincial council, of which Robert Brooke was the head.

Subsequently Governor Stone confessed that he had misapprehended the Commissioners, and they then reappointed him and his secretary, and named a council to co-operate with them, until further orders from England.

Matters now remained quiet until February the seventh, 1653–4, when Governor Stone, pursuant to instructions from Lord Baltimore, issued an order in his name, declaring that unless all persons claiming lands took the oath of fidelity to the Proprietor, and obtained patents according to the terms prescribed, they would be forever debarred from any claims to the lands on which they had settled.

This created great excitement among those settlers who had come from Nansemond, in Virginia, and their friends; men who had done more than any other to build up and give character to the colony, and Edward Lloyd and seventy-seven other persons of the housekeepers and freemen of Severn River, and Richard Preston and sixty others of Patuxent River, petitioned the Commissioners for the Commonwealth of England for relief.

It should be here noticed that about the month of August, 1652, Cecil Baltimore presented a paper to the authorities in England, showing the importance of not uniting Maryland with Virginia, to the prejudice of his patent and right to Maryland, where he maintains a deputy governor at his own charge. Strange to say, the old friend of James and Charles also urged the *cavalier* tendencies of Virginia, and claimed that *Maryland* and *New England* were the only *two provinces* that did not declare against the Parliament.[1]

"As late as December the twenty-ninth, 1653, the Council of State, upon the petition of Col. Samuel Matthews, Agent for Virginia, referred the questions between Lord Baltimore and the people of Virginia concerning their bounds, with the papers, in the hands of the Committee of the Navy, to the Lord Protector; and two days after, proclamations were ordered to be sent to Governor Richard Bennett, declaring the Government of the Commonwealth entrusted to Oliver Cromwell, Lord Protector, and successive triennial Parliaments. Lord President Henry Lawrence at the same time stated that 'his Highness has put into an effectual way the speedy resolutions of the questions between Lord Baltimore and the people of Virginia.'"

On the sixth of May, 1654, Governor Stone, by proclamation, acknowledged Cromwell as Protector of England, Scotland, and Ireland, and the government of the Proprietary as sub-

---

[1] Cal. State Papers, Col. Series, 1574–1660, p. 388.

ordinate thereto, but ignored Bennett and Clayborne as Commissioners.

The latter therefore, at Patuxent, on July the fifteenth, issued a manifesto which contained the following statement:

"Whereas we have lately received commands from his Highness, the Lord Protector, to publish the said platform of government; and that all writs and proceedings should be issued in the name of his Highness; to which though we desire this government to be conformable, yet the said Captain Stone and Mr. Hatton have lately associated unto them divers counsellors, all of the Romish religion, and excluding others appointed by the Parliament Commissioners, have and do refuse to be obedient to the constitutions thereof and to the Lord Protector therein; and have, in the name and by the special direction of the said Lord Baltimore, made proclamation and exacted an oath of fidelity from all the inhabitants of the province contrary and inconsistent to the said platform of government, which said oath nevertheless, and the law here commanding the same and many other laws, are likewise, by the report of the said Committee of the Council of State, declared to be contrary to the laws and statutes of the English nation, which is an express breach of his patent," etc. etc.

Five days after this declaration, Governor Stone resigned his power as Governor under

Baltimore, and promised to submit to such government as the Commissioners in the name of the Protector should establish, and on the twenty-second of July, Commissioners were appointed to conduct the government, and William Durand made Secretary.

The government remained in the hands of the Commissioners without disturbance until January, 1654–5, when a person, named Eltonhead, arrived in the Golden Fortune, Captain Tilghman, Commander, from England. He seems to have brought instructions from Lord Baltimore, who was dissatisfied with Stone for surrendering the government.

Stone now began to organize an armed force against the existing authorities, and, sending a party to the house of Richard Preston, on the Patuxent, the public records were seized and taken to St. Mary's, and subsequently arms and ammunition were captured from the same place. He then, with two hundred men in twelve boats, started on the twelfth of March to reduce the settlements on the Severn River. Before they reached Herring Bay, they were met by messengers in a boat from Providence with a letter of remonstrance from the authorities to Stone, and asking under what instructions he acted, and telling him "they were resolved to commit themselves into the hands of God, and rather die like men than live like slaves." The messengers were seized, but they made their escape, and told the Severn men that Stone was approaching with hostile intent. Stone also chased Captain Gookins' vessel and fired several shots. As he neared the Severn, Dr. Luke Barber, who had been in the Parliament army and attached to Cromwell's household, and had only been in Maryland four weeks, was sent with a Mr. Coursey to demand their surrender. About dusk, on the twenty-fourth of March, 1654–5, the fleet of insurgents arrived at the mouth of the Severn.

In the harbor were two vessels, the Golden Lion, a large ship, commanded by Captain Roger Heamans, and a small New England trading vessel, in charge of Captain John Cutts. When Stone's flotilla came in range, a shot was fired from the Golden Lion to halt him, but he moved on toward Horn Point, and began to land his men on this neck of land, now a suburb of Annapolis.

As the night soon came, it rendered fighting impracticable; but on the next morning, Sunday, Stone found that the creek where his boats lay was blockaded by the Golden Lion, and this vessel opening fire upon them, forced them to move up the peninsula, where they drew up in line of battle, displaying the colors of Lord Baltimore. The Severn men, to the number of one hundred and twenty, under Captain Fuller, marched around the peninsula, with the colors of the Commonwealth, and offered battle. A few scattering shots at first, killed William Ayres, the bearer of the colors of England, and this led to a general engagement. The word of the Severn men was, "In the name of God, fall on!" and that of Baltimore's men, "Hey for Saint Mary's!"

The contest was short and sharp, and Stone's party, completely routed, threw down their arms and begged for mercy.

After the battle, a court-martial was held, and as the insurgents pretended to act under no written authority from any one, Eltonhead, and Lieut. William Lewis, and two others, who had in some way rendered themselves more obnoxious than the others, were executed for treason. Mrs. Stone, in a letter to Lord Baltimore, says: "They tried all your councillors by a council of war, and sentence was passed upon my husband to be shot to death, but was after saved by the enemy's own soldiers, and so the rest of the councillors were saved by the petitions of the women, with some other friends they found there."

Soon after the battle, Governor Bennett went to England, and the Council of Virginia wrote, on June the twenty-eighth, 1655, that "they did never intermeddle between those men of Severn and my Lord Baltimore his officers, but what hath been, was by the Commissioners Richard

Bennett and Col. Will. Clayborne, authorized by the Parliament, without the consent of the Council or Assembly of Virginia. And further, that since one of the said Commissioners, Richard Bennett, is now in England employed as Agent for Virginia, and is there present to answer to this Parliament business, acted by him as Commissioner aforesaid; and that the countenancing of either party may be the occasion of further bloodshed."[1]

Colonel Bennett seems to have acquainted the Protector with the doubts of some of the Virginians, as to the propriety of the acts of the Commissioners of Maryland, and the following letter was written on September twenty-sixth, 1655, by Cromwell to settle doubts:

"It seems to us, by yours of the twenty-ninth of June, and by the relation we received by Colonel Bennett, that some mistake or scruple hath arisen concerning the sense of our letter of the twelfth of January last; as if by our letters we had intimated that we could have a stop put to the proceedings of those Commissioners who were authorized to settle the civil government of Maryland, which was not at all intended by us, nor so much as proposed to us by those who made addresses to us to obtain our said letter; but our intention was, as our said

[1] Thurloe State Papers.

letter doth plainly import, only to prevent and forbid any force or violence to be offered by either of the plantations of Virginia or Maryland from one to the other, upon the differences concerning their bounds, the said differences being then under the consideration of ourself and council here, which for your more full satisfaction we have thought fit to signify to you."

Cecil Baltimore and the Adventurers of Maryland, in January, 1655–56, made complaint to the Lord Protector against Bennett and Clayborne, for shooting four men to death in cold blood, and ask a restitution of their rights, and at the same time the Commissioners presented a counter-petition.

A pamphlet also appeared, written by a Baltimore partisan, styled: "Hammond *versus* Heamans; or, an answer to an audacious pamphlet, published by an impudent and ridiculous fellow named Roger Heamans, calling himself Commander of the ship Golden Lion, wherein he endeavors, by lies and holy expressions, to color over his murders and treacheries committed in the Province of Maryland, to the utter ruin of that flourishing plantation; having for a great sum sold himself to proceed in those cruelties; it being altogether answered out of the abstract of credible oaths taken here in England. In which is published his Highnesses absolute though neglected command to Richard Bennett, late Governor of Virginia, and all others, not to disturb the Lord Baltimore's plantation in Maryland. By John Hammond,[1] a sufferer in these calamities. Printed at London for the use of the author, and are to be sold at the Royall Exchange in Cornhill."

On the thirty-first of July, 1656, the Council of State considered the petition of Colonels Matthews and Bennett, and also the report from Lords Whitelocke and Widrington, relating to Virginia and Maryland, and recommended that the whole matter be referred to the Committee of Trade for their opinion.

This Committee having made a report, the whole matter, on December the seventeenth, was referred to the Committee on Plantations, to confer with Baltimore and the other parties, and report what they conceived fit to be done.

After many interviews, on the thirtieth of November, 1657, articles of agreement were signed by Cecil Baltimore and the Commissioners Ben-

---

[1] John Hammond for seventeen years resided in Virginia; but, in November, 1652, by an act of the Assembly, being at the time a burgess from the Isle of Wight, was expelled from the colony as a "scandalous person, and a frequent disturber of the peace of the country." (Hening.) He then went to Maryland, and, after Stone's insurrection, he escaped to England, and beside the pamphlet quoted, he wrote "Leah and Rachel," in praise of the sister colonies, which is republished in the Force Historical Tracts.

nett and Matthews, in the last of which the Lord Baltimore did promise "that he would never give his assent to the repeal of a law established heretofore in Maryland by his Lordship's consent, and mentioned in the report of the Committee for trade, whereby all persons professing to believe in Jesus Christ have freedom of conscience there."

With the understanding that the oath of fidelity was not to be pressed upon the people then resident in the province of Maryland, the Commissioners in the colony surrendered their power on March the twenty-fourth, 1657–8, and Josias Fendall was proclaimed Governor, and Philip Calvert,[1] an illegitimate son of the first Lord Baltimore, was made Secretary, and writs issued for an assembly to meet on April the twenty-seventh, 1658, at St. Leonard's.

The affairs of the colony rapidly settled, the pursuits of industry were resumed, and population increased under the more liberal interpretation of the charter, and the only mention of Lord Baltimore previous to the restoration of monarchy and the accession of Charles the Second, is an order of the Council of State to

---

[1] Stuyvesant calls him an illegitimate; Heerman says he was a half-brother of Cecil Baltimore. Burke, in his Extinct Peerage, says nothing of George Baltimore having married a second time.

apprehend Cecil Lord Baltimore, and such others as are suspected to be engaged with him in making and exporting great sums of money, and to seize all money, stamps, tools, and instruments for coining.[1]

The Commissioners Bennett and Clayborne quietly retired to their plantations in Virginia, and were respected citizens, and in 1659 Samuel Matthews, their associate, died.

In 1673 Bennett lived not far from his life-long political opponent, and both were old men. William Edmundson, the companion of the celebrated George Fox, after visiting Berkeley, went to William Wright's to hold a meeting, and Major-General Bennett and some other prominent neighbors were present. Says the preacher, in the quaint language of the Society of Friends:

"They said he spoke the truth, and were courteous. The Major-General replied he was glad to hear that there was such order among us, and would it had been so with others. He further said he was a man of great estate, and many of our friends were poor, and therefore he

---

1 Mr. George Peabody has presented to the Maryland Historical Society one or two Baltimore coins. Davis thus describes the currency: "There was a provincial coin, consisting of silver, and issued by the Proprietary, having upon one side his Lordship's arms, with the motto, Crescite et Multiplicamini; upon the other his image, with the circumscription, Cœcilius Dominus Terræ-Mariæ."

desired to contribute. He likewise asked me how I was treated by the Governor [Berkeley], having heard that I was with him. I told him he was brittle and peevish, and I could get nothing further on him. He asked me if the Governor called me dog, rogue, etc. I said no, he did not call me so. Then said he, you took him in the best humor, those being his usual terms when he is angry, for he is an enemy to every appearance of good. They were tender and loving, and we parted so, the Major-General desiring to see me at his house, which I was willing to do, and accordingly went.

"He was a solid, wise man, received the truth, and died in the same, leaving two friends his executors."

His daughter, Anna, married Theodoric Bland, a gentleman of character and high social position.

A Richard Bennett, the grandson of the Governor, in 1699 was the collector of Lord Baltimore's revenues. He became the largest slaveholder in Maryland, and was buried at Bennett's Point, in Queen Anne's County.

William Clayborne settled in the valley of the Pamunkey. After Berkeley was made Governor, at his request he was again made Secretary of Virginia, and was in 1666 a member of the Virginia Assembly. He was killed in a skirmish with the Indians at Moncock Hills, and was buried on the field.[1]

In 1699 Story, the celebrated Quaker preacher, visited a William Clayborne, on Pamunkey Neck, who was probably the son of the former.

---

[1] McSherry.

CHAPTER FOURTH.

THE SOCIETY OF FRIENDS.

CECIL BALTIMORE never contributed a shilling, as far as the public records show, toward the building of a church or school-house in the Colony of Maryland. In his dispatches he seldom makes allusion to the importance of either, and therefore it is not surprising that at the Restoration, and accession of Charles the Second to the throne, there should have been less intelligence in the province than in the other colonies. During the days of the Commonwealth there appears to have been but three clergymen in the province. The Rev. William Wilkinson, of the Church of England, who, on the first of October, 1650, obtained nine hundred acres of land on the Patuxent River, fifteen miles north of Saint Mary's, which was subsequently increased to two thousand.

In 1654 arrived Father Francis Fitz Herbert,[1] an able Jesuit and fluent preacher, whose zeal stirred up animosity, and led to his indictment for treason and sedition before Governor Fendall, Secretary Philip Calvert, and Councillors Utye, Stone, Chandler, and Baker Brooke. The court convened at St. Leonard's on October the fifth, 1658, and it was charged, that he had threatened Thomas Gerard, of the Roman Catholic faith, that he would force him to bring his family to church, and also that a few weeks before, at a muster on the Upper Patuxent, he did try to proselyte. One man testified that he heard Fitz Herbert preach at Mrs. Burke's house, and the same night Richard Games turned Roman Catholic, and brought home two books given by the priest. The Jesuit very properly answered his accusers, that he had a right to be protected while preaching and teaching, since by the very first law of the country, Holy Church within the province, should have and enjoy all her rights, liberties, and franchises, among which were preaching and teaching. "Neither imports it," said he, "what church is there meant, since, by the true intent of the Act concerning Religion, every church professing to believe in God

[1] Father Starkie seems to have been in the colony as a coadjutor, but was not active.

the Father, Son, and Holy Ghost, is accounted Holy Church."

The third clergyman was the Rev. Francis Doughty,[1] who first emigrated to New England, and then came to Long Island, and while there preached to the English-speaking members of the Reformed Church in Manhattan, now New York City.

His daughter Mary there married Adrian Vanderdonk,[2] a graduate of Leyden, and distinguished lawyer, and after his death she became the wife of Hugh O'Neal, of Patuxent, and her father appears to have lived with her.

Heerman, one of the Boundary Commissioners from New Netherlands, says that while he was dining with Philip Calvert, on Sunday, October the twelfth, 1659, "Mr. Doughty, the minister, accidentally called."

The only active religious teacher was Fitz Herbert, and generally the masses were without any moral instruction.

Amid the ferments of the Cromwellian era a society of enthusiasts originated calling themselves Friends, but stigmatized as Quakers. Disgusted with the formalism of the period, and

---

[1] Governor Stone's brother-in-law was named Francis Doughty.

[2] Vanderdonk was a lineal descendant of Adrian Van Bergen, who brought the turf-boat into Breda, and thus rescued the place from the Spaniards in 1599.

eschewing every species of ritualism, they talked much of the inner light, and Christ in the heart.

Meek in bearing, neat although peculiar in dress, plain spoken even to bluntness, fearless to the verge of foolhardiness, they proclaimed their doctrines in the face of all opposition.

In 1656 they appeared in America, and not only Virginia but Massachusetts, treated them as public enemies. Four years later Daniel Gould was beaten with thirty stripes, in the latter colony, for returning without permission, and Wenlock Christopherson sentenced to death, which drew forth from his lips these words of wisdom:

"For the last man that was put to death here, are five come in his room. If you have power to take my life from me, God can raise up the same principle in ten of his servants, and send them among you in my room."

His speech made a deep impression, and he was set at liberty, when he sought the Colony of Maryland, to be kindly received by the Preston, Thomas, and Richardson families, and was usually called Christerson. Dr. Peter Sharpe, in his will, gave to Daniel Gould, and Wenlock Christerson and wife, forty shillings each, also "for perpetual standing, a horse for the Friends in the ministry, to be placed at a convenient place for their use."

The Assembly, however, forgetting the law of

the colony, looked upon them as vagabonds and "disturbers of the peace."

But the fair-minded historian cannot disguise the fact, that under the influence of these despised people, the first great religious awakening in Maryland occurred.

One day in 1672, unexpectedly to all, there landed on the banks of the Patuxent, from a ship that had come from England, by way of Jamaica, the apostle of that peculiar people, whom Cromwell said "he could not win with gifts, honors, offices, or places," George Fox, that spiritual iconoclast whose name is identified with the religious history of the seventeenth century.

Believing that time was precious, he immediately began to preach. For four days he expounded his doctrines with singular clearness, and with a mellow voice prayed from the depths of his soul, and as a result five or six justices of the peace, and many world's people who came from curiosity, went away full of interest.

Partly by land and partly by water he hastened to the Cliffs of Calvert, and addressed another large assembly.

Crossing the bay, crowds gathered to listen, and a judge's wife was frank to say, "she had rather hear him once, than the priests a thousand times."

Returning to the Western Shore, he spoke at

the Severn, where the numbers were so great that no building was large enough to hold the audience. The next day he was at Abraham Birkhead's, six or seven miles distant, and there the Speaker of the Assembly was convinced; then mounting his horse, he rode to Dr. Peter Sharpe's, at the Cliffs of Calvert. Here was a "heavenly meeting," many of the upper sort of people present, and a wife of one of the Governor's councillors was convinced.

Some Roman Catholics came to deride, but they had no heart to oppose. From thence he rode eighteen miles to James Preston's, on the Patuxent, where an Indian chief and some of his tribe came to see the strange man who was lifting up his voice in the wilderness. After a tour to Virginia and Carolina, he came back to Preston's on the twenty-seventh of the eleventh month, 1672, and soon began to travel in the face of snow storms to declare the truth in Christ as he understood it. Taking a boat at the Cliffs for the Eastern Shore, he was obliged to pass a winter's night without fire. In Somerset County he held a meeting at Anamessex, and then proceeded to Hunger's Creek, Little Choptank, Tredhaven, Wyes, and to John Taylor's, on Kent Island.

His labors had been incessant: neither snow storms nor the burning sun had detained. He forded streams, slept in the woods and in barns with as much complacency as in the comfortable houses of his friends, and was truly a wonder unto many.

Before he returned to England he rested a few days at the Cliffs, went up to Annapolis, and attended the meeting of the Provincial Assembly, and early in 1673 sailed for his native land. Those attached to ritualism were horrified at the excitement created. On May the twenty-fifth, 1676, the Rev. John Yeo, of Patuxent, wrote to the Archbishop of Canterbury: "The Province of Maryland is in a desperate condition for the want of an established ministry. Ten or twelve counties; twenty thousand souls; three Protestant ministers of the Church. The Papists are provided for, and the Quakers take care of those that are speakers, but no care is taken to build up churches in the Protestant religion. The Lord's day is profaned, religion is despised, and all notorious vices are committed; so that it is become a Sodom of uncleanness and a pest-house of iniquity."

The Archbishop referred the letter to the Bishop of London, who called Charles Baltimore's attention to the subject, who, with great justice, replied: "The Act of 1647, confirmed in 1676, tolerates and protects every sect. Four ministers of the Church of England are in possession of plantations which afforded them a decent subsistence. That from the various religious tenets of the members of the Assembly, it would be extremely difficult, if not impossible, to induce it to consent to a law that shall oblige any sect to maintain other ministers than its own."

The four "Protestant ministers of the Church" appear to have been Yeo and Wilkinson, conformists, and Doughty and Matthew Hill, noncomformists. The latter settled in Charles County in 1669, and was a Presbyterian in his preferences. He was a native of Yorkshire, educated at Magdalen College, and considered a good Hebrew scholar. Ordained as a minister of the Church of England, he preached at Thirsk until ejected in 1662 for non-conformity. He was a quiet, judicious man, and retired to London, and there lost his all in the great fire. He subscribed one of his letters at this period, "Your brother, sine re, sine spe, tantum non sine se." He embarked for the West Indies "with a light cargo, a few clothes, a Bible, a concordance, and a small parcel of manuscript," and appears to have come from thence with some Scotch people to Maryland. His father-in-law, Walter Bayne, entered a tract of five thousand acres, called Barbadoes, on the east side of the main fresh run of Port Tobacco creek. He was useful and respected in his neighborhood, appearing on the records as Matthew Hill, gent., and seems to have been opposed to the agitations of John Coode, and left the country.[1]

The colony was now greatly disturbed by religious dissensions, the Church of England men longing for an establishment supported by law, and the Quakers and the Roman Catholics advocating the protection of all.

Lord Culpepper, Governor of Virginia, alluding to the condition of things in the adjoining colony, wrote: "Maryland is now in a ferment, and not only troubled with our disease—poverty—but in very great danger of falling in pieces; whether it be that the old Lord Baltimore's politic maxims are not followed by the son, or that they will not do in the present age, in a word, it is so far from being in a condition to assist us, that it is worthy your Lordship's prudence, to take care of Maryland."

In 1674 a petition was presented to the Colonial Assembly, signed by Richard Beard, the gentleman who made the first map of Annapolis, Wenlock Christerson, and others, asking that they might be permitted to affirm, instead of taking the oath prescribed by law. About this time, also, John Cornman was condemned to die for witchcraft, used upon the body of Elizabeth

---

[1] Calamy says after he was settled and had bright hopes, "new troubles arose. He was a good scholar, a lively preacher, and of a free and generous spirit."

Goodall. Governor Calvert, on petition of the lower house of the Assembly, ordered a reprieve, "on condition that the Sheriff of St. Mary County convey him to the gallows, and that the rope being about his neck, it be there made known to him how much he was indebted to the lower house for their intercessions, and that he should then be employed by the Governor and Council in such service as they should think fit."

Edmundson, who had been the companion of George Fox, three years after, made a second visit to Maryland.

Going in an open boat to the great Bay of Anamessex, to visit friends there, he was exposed to a cold storm, and stopped at an uninhabited island, where he stayed all night with no covering but a canvas sail. From thence, hoping to find shelter, he stood across the bay, but was out a day and night exposed to sleet and snow. Reaching Benjamin Lawrence's, on the Patuxent, he could not walk, but those that acknowledged him as their Moses, furnished an Aaron and a Hur, who stayed him up, one on the one side and the other on the other side, and after holding two meetings, he was lovingly borne back to the boat, and proceeded on a mission to Virginia.

A son of Admiral Penn, while a student at Oxford, listened to the preaching of a disciple of Fox, and convinced that if there was "no cross" there could be "no crown," embraced the tenets of the "Society of Friends," and was expelled, not only from college, but from his father's house.

Obtaining a charter from the King, he founded "a free colony for all mankind," which to this day bears his name.

Shortly after his arrival at Philadelphia, the cultivated Penn proceeded to Maryland, and visited friends on West River. Charles Baltimore met him, with an escort of the Councillors of the colony, and Colonel Taillor, Deputy Surveyor-General, extended the hospitalities of his mansion at the Ridge of Anne Arundel County.

Penn from thence went back to William Richardson's on West River, and attended a religious meeting at Thomas Hooker's, two miles distant.

Subsequently, about the year 1700, while John Richardson was preaching at yearly meeting at Tredhaven, on the Eastern Shore, William Penn and Charles Lord Baltimore and wife arrived.

Richardson describes the wife as "a notable, wise, natural and courteously-carriaged woman." She was much disappointed that the meeting was soon to close, and she told Penn that she did not wish to hear him, and such as he, for he was a scholar, but she would like to listen to the expositions of some of the unlearned mechanics and husbandmen.

In 1691, the good John Wilson, on his way from a mission to Virginia and Carolina, "after traveling all day, sat down in the dark of the evening to eat some bread and cheese." In his journal he writes: "We lodged that night in the woods, and as soon as the day broke, set forward on our journey northward, and met with two men, one of whom, being an ancient, comely man, kindly invited us to his house, where we stayed two nights, and had a meeting, though he was an elder among the Presbyterians.

"He also lent us his boat to go over the Potomac, and that night we lodged at a poor man's house, and had no bed to lie on. We got next day over Pautuxent River."

In 1699, Thomas Story, who was the Paul among the Friends of America, came from Philadelphia, teaching and preaching in the wilderness of Maryland.

Receiving in England the education of a cavalier, he was skilled in the arts of fencing and music, and a proficient in Greek and mathematical studies. His early associations were with High Churchmen. The church he attended in youth, conformed to the minutest prescriptions of Laud. The minister in public prayer turned his face toward the east, and the congregation bowed the knee at the name of Jesus. His brother, moreover, was Chaplain of the Countess of Carlisle.

For a time he was zealous in the observance of rites, but before long questioned their propriety, and at length bounded over to the Society, which abnegated all ritualism. He emigrated to Pennsylvania, and being a lawyer by profession, was made Master of the Rolls and Keeper of the Great Seal of the Colony, and subsequently Mayor of the City of Philadelphia.

After making a religious visit to Virginia, he crossed the Potomac at Cedar Point, and on arriving in Maryland, was politely entertained by William Herbert, a member of the Church of England, and then went to Cool Spring,[1] where many diseased people were, on account of the medicinal quality of the water, and he preached to them in a large tobacco house. Reaching the Patuxent at Benedict, he crossed, and visited Elizabeth Hutchins, at the Cliffs of Calvert. From thence he proceeded to Samuel Galloway's,[2] at the Ridge, whose wife was the only preacher in those parts.

---

[1] Among the early laws of the province, is "An act to purchase lands adjoining the fountains of healing waters, called the Cool Springs, and for building houses for the entertainment of such poor and impotent persons as shall repair thither for cure."

[2] The Galloways came to Maryland prior to 1640. Joseph Shippen, Secretary of Province of Pennsylvania, married, Sept. 29, 1768, Jane, daughter of John Galloway, of Ann Arundel Co., Maryland.

On the twenty-seventh day of the third month, O.S., 1699, he attended yearly meeting at West River, in company with Dr. Griffith Owen, of Philadelphia.[1] On the thirtieth, his journal tells us, "came one Henry Hall, a priest of the Church of England, and with others of his notion, eaves-dropped the meeting, but came not in." Richard Johns, seizing a proper occasion, arose and pronounced the following Catholic confession of faith, a slight modification of the Apostles' Creed:

"We believe that the Lord Jesus Christ, who was born of the Virgin Mary, being conceived by the promise and influence of the Holy Ghost, is the true Messiah or Saviour; that he died upon the cross at Jerusalem, a propitiation and sacrifice for the sins of all mankind; that he rose from the dead on the third day, ascended, and seated on the right hand of the Majesty on high, making intercession for us; and in the fullness of time shall come to judge both the living and the dead, and reward all according to their work."

The priest dissatisfied, went off, but came the next day and eaves-dropped.

"My companion, in his testimony, apprehend-

---

[1] Dr. Griffith Owen was much beloved by Penn. In his letters he calls him "tender Griffith Owen." He was skillful in his profession, and died much lamented, in 1717.

ing they were within hearing," continues Story, "cried aloud to them to come forth out of their holes, and appear openly like men, and if they had anything to say after meeting was over, they should be heard."

Story then publicly challenged them to prove their call to the ministry, "which they taking upon them to do, only told us that Christ called apostles, and they ordained others, and they again others in succession to that time."

"Then I called for their proof who they were that the apostles ordained, and who from age to age successors ordained, wherein if they justly failed they were to be rejected as no ministers of Christ, since they had rested the matter on such a succession.

"Many of the people seeing their ignorance said: 'We'll pay you the tobacco, being obliged by law, that is forty pounds of tobacco for every negro slave, but we will never hear you more.'

"While we were yet in the gallery one climbed up into a window, and cried out with a loud voice to Henry Hall, 'Sir, you have broken a canon of the Church, you have baptized several negroes, who, being infidels, baptism ought not to have been administered to them.'[1]

---

[1] In 1715 the Assembly enacted the following law: "Forasmuch as many people have neglected to baptize their negroes, or to suffer them to be baptized, on a vague apprehension that

"At this the priest was enraged, but made no answer to the charge, only fumed and fretted, and threatened the man to trounce him. Then I observed to the people, that if these negroes were made Christians in this sense, members of Christ, children of God, inheritors of the Kingdom of Heaven, received into the body of the Church of Christ, as the language is at the time of sprinkling, how could they now detain them longer as slaves?

"Several justices of the peace being ashamed of their priest, slid out of the meeting as unobservable as might be, and the people in general contemned them as such, who behind the back of the Quakers had greatly reproached and belied them, but face to face were utterly subdued by them. That night several of the justices, lodging with our friend Samuel Chew, expressed their sentiments altogether in our favor, and that the priests were really ignorant men in matters of religion."

At a later period Story made a tour on the Eastern Shore with Edward Shippen[1] and wife,

---

negroes by receiving sacrament of baptism are manumitted or set free;

"Be it hereby further declared and enacted, that no negro, or negroes, by receiving the holy sacrament of baptism is thereby manumitted or set free, nor hath any right or title to manumission more than he or they had before, any law, usage, or custom to the contrary notwithstanding."

[1] Edward Shippen came to Boston in 1675, and was whipped

Samuel Carpenter,[1] Isaac Norris,[2] and Griffith Owen. At Little Choptank he had a public discussion with a minister of the Church of England, and from thence to Edward Fisher's, at Nanticoke, where the King's attorney disputed with him. Crossing at a ferry on the Pocomoke, the party arrived at widow Mary Johnson's, on

---

for his opinions on the Common, and then moved to Philadelphia. His last wife was Anna Francina, daughter of Matthias Vanderheyden, near Bohemia River, Md. In 1706 his daughter, Anna, was married to Thomas Story.

Gabriel Thomas, in an account of the Province of Pennsylvania, published at London, in 1698, says:

"Edward Shippey has an orchard and gardens adjoining his great house that equalize any I have ever seen, having a very pleasant and famous summer-house erected in the middle of his garden, abounding with tulips, pinks, carnations, roses, lilies, not to mention those that grew wild in the fields." Tradition says he was distinguished for three things, "being the biggest man, and having the biggest house, and the biggest carriage in the place." His grandson was Chief Justice of Pennsylvania, whose daughter wrecked herself, by marrying the traitor Benedict Arnold.

An Edward Shippen, one of his descendants, appears in the last Naval Register as a surgeon U. S. N.

[1] Samuel Carpenter was considered the wealthiest man in the city. He built the house that William Penn occupied when he visited the province, and is still standing, on Second above Walnut Street. He was Treasurer of the province, and died in 1713.

[2] Isaac Norris was Chief Justice of the Province of Pennsylvania, and his house and garden occupied the ground on Chestnut and Fifth Streets, now occupied by the U. S. Custom-house, Post-office, and Philadelphia Library.

Muddy Creek, and on the next first day of the week there was preaching to a large congregation in the meeting-house. That night they all rode to the house of Thomas Fooks,[1] at Onancock, in Accomac County, Virginia, and the next morning started for Naswadox Creek,[2] twenty-five miles below, in Northampton, and had a large meeting at the meeting-house.

Returning to Muddy Creek, they rode from there to George Truitt's,[3] in Maryland, where they stayed and held a meeting; then went to Walter Lane's, fifteen miles off, where the meeting was small, a court being held at the same time.

Next they were at Thomas Evernden's, at "Anomessicks," where they remained two days, and on the fourth day of the sixth month they came to Richard Waters's, where the meeting "was hard and dry." Then proceeding to the bay, one of their number took a sloop for the

---

[1] Francis Makemie, the Presbyterian clergyman in the early days of the colony, used to preach at the house of Thomas Fooks.

[2] Naswadox was the residence of the Browns and Upshurs, Quakers, the ancestors of Abel P. Upshur, once Secretary of the Navy.

George Keith, in 1701, published "An Occasional Conference with Thomas Upshare."

[3] George Truitt's was probably near Snow Hill. There still exists an old Quaker grave-yard about five miles above that place, on the road that leads to Berlin.

Western Shore, and the rest rode thirty miles to George Truitt's. The next day a journey of thirty-five miles was made to Cedar Creek, and the following morning crossed the inlet at Atkinson's, saving seven miles, and reached Lewes in the evening, and visited William Clarke,[1] who gave out notice for a meeting on the next day.

In 1702 Samuel Bownas, of England, the father-in-law of Joshua Nicholson, arrived at the Patuxent, on the twenty-ninth day of the fifth month, O. S., and attended yearly meeting at West River.

This meeting had become one of the established institutions of the colony, and its annual occurrence was eagerly looked for by all classes and conditions of society. Young men from all parts of the colony flocked thither with fine horses to compare them, and give a trial of their speed; others came to look at the beautiful and pure-minded maidens, who in their plain drab silks and scooped bonnets, were only the more lovely in the eyes of their admirers.

Families from different counties, rolled there in their carriages, for the purpose of social reunions; and merchants of the province came to make their bargains and contracts for the year.

---

[1] William Clarke was a lawyer, and afterward moved to Philadelphia, and built an expensive house, called Clarke's Hall, which stood on the site of the Girard Bank, nearly opposite the Philadelphia Exchange.

It being near Whitsuntide, the black slaves flocked there to enjoy rest from the hardships of a tobacco plantation, for a few days. Edmundson well observed: "Yearly meeting in Maryland, many people resort to it, and transact a deal of trade with one another, so that it is a kind of market or 'change, where the captains of ships, and the planters meet and settle their affairs, and this draws abundance of people."

The crowds became so great in time, that it was necessary to check the evil, and protect the quiet Friends by legislation.[1]

---

[1] In 1725 a protective law was enacted, with the following preamble:

"Whereas, it is humbly represented to this General Assembly, by the people called Quakers, that sundry persons set up booths, and sell drinks and other things near their yearly meetings, whereby their places which were by them intended and used as places of solemn worship are converted into places of traffic, debauchery, and immorality, to their very great disturbance in the exercise of their religion and worship of God, and forasmuch as the several methods used for the suppression of such irregularities have proved altogether insufficient, it is humbly prayed that it may be enacted."

In 1747 they again petitioned that, notwithstanding the existing laws, "they, as well as those of other persuasions who resort to their yearly meetings, labor under and suffer many inconveniences from the great concourse of idle and profligate white people, and great crowds of negroes, that assemble together at the usual times of their yearly meetings, held at their meeting-houses, drinking to excess, and behaving in a rude and turbulent manner, at booths and other places where strong and spirituous drinks can be had, and that they have for

As settlements were few, Edmundson necessarily traveled over the same route as his predecessors.

The historian is under obligation to him, for preserving an account of the Society of the followers of Labadie,[1] which once existed on the banks of Chester River. Early in August, 1702, with a companion, he visited the settlement, and was courteously treated.

"When supper came in, it was placed upon a long table in a large room, where, when all things were ready, about twenty men or upwards came in at a call, but no women.

"We all sat down, they placing me and my companion near the head of the table, and having paused a short space, one pulled off his hat,

---

some years been put to very great inconvenience, and endangered in passing and repassing to and from their said meeting-house in Talbot County, by multitudes of rude and disorderly people, that gather together to run horse-races, on the road between Talbot meeting-house and Thirdhaven Creek, near a place called New Market."

The petition was answered by an enactment forbidding any one, during yearly meetings, to race horses within five miles of the meeting-houses at West River and in Talbot County.

[1] Jean de Labadie was born in 1610, and was a Jesuit. In 1650 he became a Protestant, and settled at Montauban. He then went to Geneva, and in 1666 was invited to Middleburg, Holland, and the princess palatine, Elizabeth, became one of his followers. For his mysticism, he was deposed by the Synod of Naarden, and he then founded the sect known as Labadists.

but not the rest till a short space after; and then one after another they all pulled their hats off, and as that occurred sat silent, uttered no words that we could hear for half or quarter of an hour; and as they did not uncover at once, so did they neither cover again at once, but as they put on their hats fell to eating, not regarding those who were still uncovered, so that it might be two minutes' time or more between the first and last putting off their hats.

"I afterward queried with my companion concerning the reason of their conduct, and he gave for this answer that they held it unlawful to pray, till they felt some inward motive for the purpose, and that secret prayer was more acceptable than to utter words. I likewise queried if they had no women among them. He told me they had, but the women all by themselves; having all things in common respecting their household affairs, so that none could claim any more right than another to any part of the stock; all men, whether rich or poor, must put what they had in the common stock, and likewise if they had a mind to leave, they must go out empty-handed.

"They frequently expound the Scriptures among themselves; and being a very large family, in all upward of one hundred men, women, and children, they carried on the manufacturing of linen, and had a very large plantation of corn, tobacco, flax, and hemp, together with cattle of several kinds."

In many respects, resembling the Moravians, yet like the majority of communist organizations, they were short-lived, and when Bownas, twenty-five years after, visited America, there was not a vestige left. During the second tour he visited the lower counties of the Eastern Shore, going from Choptank to Nanticoke, crossing the Vienna Ferry to Mulberry Grove, and from thence to the Widow Gale's at Monay. Then he journeyed to Annamessex and Virginia. "One Captain Drummond desired a meeting at his house. He was a Judge of the Court and sensible man." He went from thence to "Edward Mifflin's, who was a firm and zealous elder," who took him in his boat across the Bay to Nansemond.

The Church of England men, wincing from the logical arguments of Story's legal mind, through Sir Thomas Lawrence, the spendthrift Secretary of the colony, under Governor Nicholson, complained of what they called his tart expressions to the Lords of Trade and Plantations.

William Penn being in England, his attention was called to the charges, and thus alludes to the matter in a letter to a friend:

"A silly knight! Though I hope it comes of officious weakness, the talent of the gentleman, with some malice, matters there are never attacked by Thomas Story, nor in irreverent tones. I never heeded it; only said that if the gentleman had sense enough for his office, he might have known this tale was no part of it: that Thomas Story was discreet and temperate, and did not exceed in his retort or returns.

"But 'tis children's play to provoke a combat, and then cry out that such a one beats them.

"That I hoped they were not a committee of conscience and religion, and that it showed the shallowness of the gentleman, that played the busy-body in it."

Never had the colony flourished so much as during the period when the Quakers were influential. They were cleanly in their habits, industrious, intelligent, and domestic; not given to wine or brawling, and honest in their mercantile transactions. The Lloyds and others of the Society had credit at London, and they exercised a powerful influence in bringing to the colony some of the best families in the land. Here Pemberton[1] and Richard Hill, who were among Penn's right-hand men, and others afterward prominently identified with the Pennsylvania Colony, first landed.

The population, which in 1676 was estimated at twenty thousand, in 1704 was thirty-five thou-

---

[1] Pemberton became Surveyor-General of Pennsylvania, and one of his descendants was the Major-General who so long withstood General Grant at Vicksburg.

Salisbury was laid out on the lands, that once belonged to a Widow Pemberton, who may have been of the same race.

sand; four thousand four hundred and seventy-five of which were slaves.

The annual income of Lord Baltimore from the ground rents now exceeded ten thousand dollars, and was rapidly increasing.

CHAPTER FIFTH.

BOUNDARY DISPUTES.

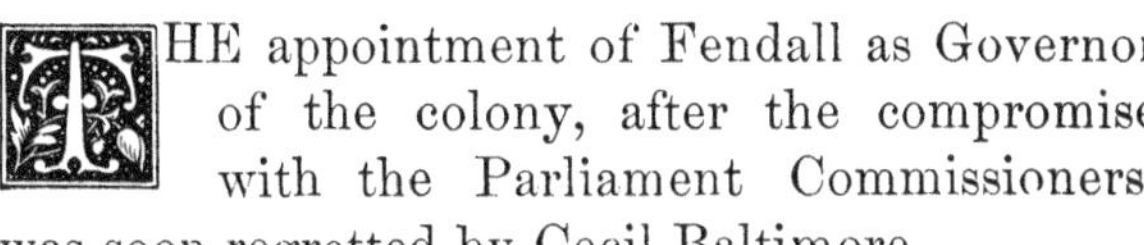

THE appointment of Fendall as Governor of the colony, after the compromise with the Parliament Commissioners, was soon regretted by Cecil Baltimore.

The Assembly convened at Thomas Gerard's, on February twenty-eighth, 1659, and the lower house, on March the first, adjourned to Robert Slye's, and on the twelfth of the month addressed the following note:

"To the Honorable the Governor and Council:

"That this Assembly of Burgesses, judging themselves to be a lawful assembly, without dependence on any other power in the province now in being, is the highest court of judicature. And if any objection can be made to their continuing, we desire to hear it."

The next day Governor Fendall replied, that he thought it had been the intention of the King, when he gave the patent to Lord Baltimore, that the freemen of the province should make their own laws, provided they conformed to reason, and the statutes of England. Gerard and Utye, with the Governor, assented to the position of the lower house, and it was then declared that the upper house should no longer sit as a distinct body.

Fendall was immediately elected President, and he and his councillors accepted new commissions from the Assembly, as the source of power.

During this period, active efforts were made to absorb the Dutch settlements on the Delaware. De Vries and others had planted colonies on the banks of that river, long before Baltimore sought for a patent. The Dutch were first at Hoarkill, now Lewistown. In 1623 Fort Nassau, near Gloucester, N. J., was built; and ten years later, Corsen went from thence, in company with Augustine Heerman and others, and purchased of the Indians the site of Philadelphia, and erected near the mouth of the Schuylkill, Fort Beversrede.

In 1635, fourteen or fifteen persons, under Capt. George Holmes, from Maryland or Virginia, seized Fort Nassau, but subsequently were captured by the Dutch, taken to Manhattan, and sent to Virginia.[1] Seven years afterward, the English from Maryland took possession near the mouth of the Schuylkill, and the sloops Real and St. Martin were sent from Manhattan to assist in dislodging them.[2]

---

[1] De Vries. [2] Acrelius.

In 1656, the burgomasters of Amsterdam determined to garrison New Amstel, or New Castle, and a company of soldiers were dispatched, under Captain Creager and Lieutenant Alexander D'Hyniossa, who had long served in Brazil. They arrived at the Delaware in the following May, and Captain Creager shortly after visited Kent Island, and there learned that the authorities of Maryland were becoming jealous of their increasing numbers. In the year 1659, the trading ports of the Dutch were at Hoarkill (Lewes), New Amstel (New Castle), and Passayung (Philadelphia), and Governor Fendall sent Colonel Nathaniel Utye to command them to depart forthwith from his Lordship's province.

The New Netherlanders were surprised at the tone of this dispatch, and sent two of their best men, Augustine Heerman and Resolved Waldron, to confer with the Maryland authorities. Reaching Kent Island on October third, they passed the night at Capt. Wickes', and on the seventh were at Billingsly's Plantation, on the Cliffs, and then went to Coursey's, on the Patuxent, and leaving their boat, walked nine miles to Philip Calvert's, the Secretary of the colony, and after a brief visit, went to the house of Overzee, the next neighbor, and a fellow-countryman of the Commissioners, to lodge.

On the next Sunday, the Commissioners, with Mr. Overzee, dined with Philip Calvert, and on the sixteenth went to Mr. Bateman's, on the Patuxent, twenty miles distant, to meet the Council of the colony. A dinner party was here given to the strangers. At the table, Heerman sat on the left of Gov. Fendall, and Philip Calvert on the right, and Mr. Waldron next. After dinner, the Commissioners presented a paper to the Council, recounting the various steps they had taken in settling the Delaware, and stated that they had maintained friendly correspondence with Virginia and Maryland until the eighth of September, 1659, when Col. Nat. Utye came to South River into the town and Fort New Amstel, and in a commanding manner and strange way, demanded that the place and country should be delivered up; and then concluded with "wishing God Almighty to conduct them to all prudent results, so that we may live neighborly together."

In the course of the discussion, Utye lost his temper, and the Governor was obliged to interpose. In the evening, harmony appears to have been restored, as it passed in taking a glass of wine and general conversation.

The visit of the Commissioners did not tend to the solution of the questions in dispute, and the next year Capt. James Neale, of Maryland, as the attorney of Lord Baltimore, appeared before the directors of the West India Company, in Amsterdam, to urge the claims of the proprietor.

In the year 1661, Edmund Scarburgh,[1] John Elzey, and Randall Rouell were authorized to induce settlers from the peninsula of Virginia to dwell in the valley of the Pocomoke and adjoining territory. In a few months, settlements were begun at Manokin and Annamessex. Scarburgh at length claimed that the country was a part of Virginia, arrested Elzey, and constrained the settlers to acknowledge Virginia jurisdiction.

These acts were disclaimed by Berkeley, and Philip Calvert on the part of Maryland, and Scarburgh as Surveyor General of Virginia, on the twenty-fifth of July, 1668, agreed upon a boundary, an east line from the extreme part of the most western angle of Watkins Point over Pocomoke River, and thence over Swansecute's Creek into the marsh of the seaside. The southern boundary of the Eastern Shore being settled by agreement, encouragement was given to settlements near Lewes, on Delaware Bay, and Col. Wm. Stevens was authorized to induce emigrants to take up land in that vicinity.

In the year 1663 a report was brought to Beeckman, one of the Dutch officers on the

---

[1] Scarburgh, from the year 1630, had been prominent as a representative of Accomac County, Va. His daughter married Custis, formerly an innkeeper at Rotterdam, and the ancestor of the first husband of Mrs. George Washington.

Judge George P. Scarburgh, formerly of U. S. Court of Claims, now of Norfolk, Va., is a descendant.

Delaware, that Charles Calvert, Governor of Maryland, was about to visit Altona, and finding "that here on the river not a single draught of French wine is obtainable," requests Stuyvesant to send him some from Manhattan to treat the nobleman.

On the ninth of August Calvert visited New Amstel and Altona, with an escort of twenty-six or seven persons, and, with Van Sweringen as Commissioner on the part of the Dutch, renewed the treaty with the Indians.

He was very favorably impressed by the kind conduct of the Dutchmen, and with the best feeling returned to Maryland, expressing his intention to visit Boston next spring, by the way of Manhattan.

Early in 1664, while England and Holland were at peace, a squadron, under Colonel Nichols, was fitted out by the Duke of York to reduce New Netherlands. D'Hyniossa sent word to Stuyvesant, at Manhattan, that he would send him five thousand pounds of powder if needed, to aid in the defense of the settlements, but all efforts were useless, and the whole province was soon subdued, Sir Robert Carr visiting the settlements on the Delaware River and compelling them to surrender.

Heerman, Van Sweringen, and others then retired, and became good citizens of the Maryland Colony.

There is still preserved the following letter from D'Hyniossa, late Director at New Castle, written from the house of Captain Thomas Howell, at Saint Marys, to Colonel Nichols, who became Governor of New Netherland, now known as New York:

"Your honor's very agreeable answer to my letters came safely here, and I learn from it that your honor is sorry for my loss. If your honor would please to console me therein it can be done by [giving me] the rest of my lost estate, and could I get it back I am resolved to live under your honor's government, yea, on the same conditions that I had from the City of Amsterdam; meanwhile, should your honor incline thereunto the answer should be sent to me at Captain Thomas Howell's, in Maryland, where I shall still remain two or three months. Should these not be accepted by your honor, I would hereby respectfully request you to send me a letter under your honor's hand to his Highness the Duke of York, in order that I may take occasion to apply in London to his Highness aforesaid on the subject."

Nichols paid no attention to this respectful petition, but on April the tenth, 1666, in a communication to the Home Government, recommended that D'Hyniossa's Island, in the Delaware River, be given to Sir Robert Carr, in appreciation of the services rendered in the reduction, and shortly after D'Hyniossa was settled on Foster's Island, in the Chesapeake, attached to Talbot County, while Augustine Heerman, since 1660, had been the owner of Bohemia Manor.[1]

In the Grenville Library is the only map ever made by Faithorne, an artist distinguished for crayon portraits and delicate copper-plate engraving. On it is this statement: "Virginia and Maryland; as it is planted and inhabited this present year 1670: surveyed and drawn by Augustus Hermann Bohemiensis;" also a beautiful portrait of the original settler of Bohemia Manor.

In 1671 a person by the name of Jones, with others from Somerset County, surprised Lewis-

---

[1] In 1666 Augustine "Harman, of Prague, in the Kingdom of Bohemia," petitioned the Maryland Assembly for the naturalization of himself, his sons Ephraim, Georgius, Casparus, and his daughters Anna, Margaritta, Judith, and Francina.

In 1671 Alexander D'Hyniossa, of Foster's Island, of the County of Talbot, asked that he, and Margaritta, his wife, and Alexander, John, Peter, Maria, Johanna, Christina, and Barbara might be naturalized. This old soldier afterward returned to Holland, and engaged in the war with Louis the Fourteenth.

An examination of the laws of Maryland shows that among others at this period, from 1666 to 1684, the following were naturalized: John Jarbo, of Dijon, France, Peter Bayard, Arnoldus De la Grange, Desjardins, Nicholas Fountaine, of Somerset, William Blakenstein, of St. Mary, De Costa, Han Hanson, Cornelius Comegys, Axel Stillé, Jacobson, Erickson, Peterson, Le Count, Garret Van Swearingen.

town, on the Delaware, and Governor Lovelace, of New York, who claimed jurisdiction, remonstrated.

On the nineteenth of November, 1675, Lord Cecil Baltimore died, and Governor Charles Calvert being heir, went to England. Returning in 1681, he discovered that Fendall was again restless. In a letter to the Earl of Anglesea, dated July the nineteenth, he writes: "Some ill-disposed persons here, have been tampering to stir up the people of Maryland, and the northern part of Virginia to mutiny, but having notice of the chief contrivers of the design, I gave orders to apprehend Josias Fendall and John Coode, two rank Baconists."

The controversy concerning the right to a portion of the west shore of the Delaware, was now transferred from the New Netherlands, to one of Baltimore's own countrymen, a man who was his peer in birth, education, pecuniary resources, and court influence.

As soon as Penn arrived in America he proposed a conference with Lord Baltimore relative to boundaries. The meeting took place in December, 1682, at the Ridge of Ann Arundel. Penn perceiving an amanuensis taking notes of all that was said, without any previous agreement, called the attention of Baltimore to the matter, who assured him that what was uttered, would not be divulged. The promise, however, was forgotten, and as a copy of the proceedings were never submitted to him for revision, Penn called it an "unfair practice."

The following spring the two Proprietaries had a second conference at New Castle, which was more satisfactory. Baltimore wanted to talk privately, but Penn desired everything done in council and in writing. The former at last evaded the whole subject, by saying "he was not well, and the weather sultry," and asking a postponement.

Before the second meeting Baltimore had issued a proclamation granting lands to settlers around Lewistown. Penn did not know it, until after the conference at New Castle, and procuring a copy of the proclamation, sent messengers to Maryland to ask an explanation.

At first Baltimore denied any knowledge of the proclamation, then turning to two gentlemen of his council who stood by, he asked them if they remembered any such thing? They also denied it. "Upon which," says Penn, "the persons I sent produced the attested copy, which refreshing their memories, they confessed. But the Lord Baltimore told them that it was his ancient form, and he only did it to renew his claim, not that he would encourage any to plant there. Then they prayed him to call it in, lest any trouble should ensue, but he refused it."

On the seventeenth of September, 1683, Charles

Baltimore commissioned his "dear cousin," Colonel George Talbot, to repair "to the Skulkill, at Delaware," and demand all the land lying on the west side of Delaware River south of the fortieth degree of latitude.

About five miles from New Castle Talbot erected a small fort, and refused to depart, saying that he would kill all that should attempt to destroy the block-house. In reply to Talbot's demands, Penn prepared an able paper, in which he said that Charles Lord Baltimore "hath sent me letters of a very coarse style, such as indeed could not be answered without those terms, which unbecome those in public stations."

William Penn, on the eighth of June, 1684, writes from Philadelphia to the Duke of York, in allusion to Talbot's incursion, and Baltimore's departure for England:

"How far these practices will please the King or Duke it is not fit for me to say, but if not mistaken I shall be able to make evident by law he hath almost cancelled his allegiance to the King herein, and exposed himself to his mercy for all he hath in this world.

"I hear he is gone for England, and was so just as to invite me, by a letter in March, delivered in the end of April, informing me that toward the end of March he intended for England. This was contrived that he might get the start of me, that making an interest before I arrived, he might block up my way and carry the point. But such arts will never do where there is no matter to work upon, which I am abundantly satisfied they will not, they cannot, find in the Duke, with whom I know he hath great reason to ingratiate his cause. I am following him as fast as I can."

Charles Baltimore hastened to England under many apprehensions, for it was the first time since the family was ennobled that the Proprietor of the colony had not powerful friends at Court. Charles the Second was disposed to restrict rather than concede privileges, not only requiring that the officers of the colony should be Protestants, but complaining of opposition to the collectors of the customs in the execution of their duty, "after the many favors which had been heaped upon him and his father."

His affairs were rendered still more complicated by an occurrence in 1684: Christopher Rousby was the King's Collector-General in Maryland, and Colonel Talbot, Baltimore's cousin, coming on board of his Majesty's ketch, the Quaker, at the capes of Virginia, approached Rousby in a friendly manner, and taking a favorable opportunity, stabbed and killed him. The captain of the vessel immediately seized and ironed Talbot. When the intelligence reached the Council of Maryland they deputed two of their body to demand his delivery. The captain asked in whose name the requisition was made, and they replied in that of Lord Baltimore. But he refused to deliver his prisoner to any but the King's justices, and as they persisted in saying that the Proprietor was their king, he sailed away, and Talbot was taken to Virginia, tried in April, 1686, and found guilty of murder, but the next year was pardoned by the King.

Upon Baltimore's arrival in England, James the Second was on the throne, and although the Proprietary was a Roman Catholic, Edward Petre, a Jesuit, the friend and confessor of the King, proved an opponent. The Proprietor of Pennsylvania after a few months, also appeared in England, and both were for some time busy in collecting evidence by which they might strengthen their claims.

Frequently they came before the Committee of Plantations, and in the journal of its proceedings is the following entry, dated October the seventeenth, 1685:

"My Lord Baltimore and Mr. Penn were called in, and my Lord Baltimore having undertaken to procure an authenticated copy of a report made by the Committee for Foreign Plantations on the fourth day of April, 1638, touching the differences between my Lord Baltimore's predecessors and William Clayborne about the Isle of Kent, my Lord Baltimore declared he cannot find the original, whereby an attested copy may be produced; their Lordships agree to report their opinion that the tract of land now in dispute does not belong to my Lord Baltimore." At a subsequent meeting in November they declared, "that for avoiding further difficulty the tract of land lying between the River and Bay of Delaware, and the Eastern Sea on the one side, and Chesapeake Bay on the other, be divided into two equal parts by a line from the latitude of Cape Henlopen to the fortieth degree of northern latitude; and that one-half thereof lying between the Bay of Delaware and the Eastern Sea be adjudged to belong to his Majesty, and that the other half remain to the Lord Baltimore as comprised within his charter."

Matters here rested until 1732, when negotiations were renewed, and the controversy was not finally settled until July the fourth, 1760, when Frederick Lord Baltimore, and Richard and John Penn perfected terms of agreement.

CHAPTER SIXTH.

REVOLUTION OF 1689—ESTABLISHED CHURCH OF THE COLONY, AND PRESBYTERIANISM.

ITUS OATES, once a worthless clergyman of the Church of England, and subsequently an inmate of a Jesuit College on the Continent, constructed an alarming fiction, that the Pope had intrusted the Government of England to the Jesuits, who had appointed priests and Roman Catholic noblemen and gentlemen to all the highest offices in Church and State, and among his black list of conspirators was included the name of Charles Lord Baltimore.[1]

In addition to the opposition of Father Petre, the Proprietary was obliged to bear the odium of this calumny among the populace. As he rode to and from the meetings of the Committee of Trade and Plantations, to discuss the boundary question with William Penn, he could see the excited crowd talking about Oates, now on

[1] Hepworth Dixon's Penn.

trial at Westminster Hall, whose short neck, purple cheeks, low forehead, and crooked legs, stamped him as a villain of the lowest order.

Two years later, James determined to destroy the charter of Maryland, and the Attorney-General was ordered to prepare a quo-warranto, which was hindered by a change of dynasty.

In the midst of the political dissensions which arose, and led to the Revolution of 1689, Baltimore from conviction sided with the Jacobites, against the Prince of Orange. But it is said that he immediately gave in his adherence to William and Mary, after the flight of James, and dispatched orders to have their accession to the throne proclaimed by his deputies. These instructions never seemed to have arrived—not, at least, until the new sovereigns had been joyfully recognized in the sister colonies. Moreover, when the authorities heard of the invasion of England by the Prince of Orange, they had deemed it expedient to gather the public arms, scattered in the different counties, and imprisoned several persons, who were accused of attempts to excite disturbance. The motives for these acts by aspirants for power, were greatly distorted.

The watchword of the dominant party in England was "No Popery," and a few artful demagogues in the Province of Maryland echoed the cry, and industriously worked upon the passions and fears of the scattered and ignorant planters. It is possible,

> "Some truth there was, but dash'd and brew'd with lies."[1]

By a singular coincidence, the head of the revolution in Maryland was John Coode, who, like Titus Oates, had been ordained as a minister of the Church of England, but was wholly destitute of character and respectability. Said a cotemporary: "It will be an extraordinary thing when these governments are without such sort of persons as Coode, who I think is a democratic Ferguson in principles of government; an Hobbist or worse in principles of religion. It was his maxim, 'If much dirt is thrown, some of it will stick.'"[2]

About the middle of March, 1689, a false report was circulated, that the Indians were at the head of the Patuxent with hostile intentions, and on this pretext Coode and his associates, demanded arms and ammunition of the authorities, which were readily granted.

Although it was soon ascertained that there was not the slightest truth in the rumor, the less intelligent had become suspicious, and every night those that were devout, prayed to be delivered from the tomahawk of the savage and their Papal coadjutors.

---

[1] Dryden. [2] Gov. Nicholson, in Chalmers.

In April was formed "An association in arms for the defence of the Protestant religion, and for asserting the rights of King William and Queen Mary to the Province of Maryland and all the English dominions," of which Coode was the leading spirit; and a pamphlet was issued from the press[1] of Richard Cuthead, at Saint Mary's, filled with the most reckless charges against the Proprietary and his deputies.

On the sixteenth of July, a messenger came to Henry Darnall,[2] at Mattapany, one of the councillors of the colony, and stated that Coode was raising an armed force on the Potomac. Colonel Digges, of Saint Mary's, gathered together one hundred men to resist those that were marching toward the place; but he was compelled by the superior numbers of Coode to surrender the town and records.

The factionists, taking some cannon out of a ship from London, that was in the river, pro-

---

[1] The first printing press and earliest pamphlet published in the province.

[2] Davis, in "Day-star of Freedom," says: "The Darnalls, of London, arrived about twenty years before the Protestant Revolution. Colonel Henry Darnall, the emigrant, was the son of Philip Darnall, and a kinsman of Lord Baltimore. He resided at the 'Wood Yard,' in Prince George County, and at a later period at Portland Manor, in Anne Arundel. His tombstone is at the Wood Yard. The vane upon the housetop, the wainscotted wall, the other relics and memorials relating to the era of the Darnalls, are all preserved with the most studious care."

ceeded to Mattapany, the Government House, which was near to the brick mansion that had been built by Lord Charles Baltimore for a residence, and demanded its delivery. To keep awake the fears of their adherents, the leaders of the insurgents employed a man to ride up post-haste, with a letter stating that the neighboring Indians had cut their corn and disappeared from their villages, and that an Englishman had been found disemboweled. After Mattapany was given up, the Council of Maryland endeavored to send a letter by a ship captain to London, but he declined to be the bearer. A summons was now sent by the successful party to the freemen of the province to elect burgesses for an Assembly. The men of note, and men of estate, disregarded the demand. "The County of Ann Arundel, which is accounted the most populous, and richest of the whole province, and wherein is but one Papist family, unanimously stood out, and would not elect any burgesses."[1] On the third of August the Assembly met, at the house of Philip Lynes, at the head of Britton Bay, and Michael Taney,[2] the Sheriff of Calvert County, was brought before them on the third of September, and imprisoned

[1] Narrative of Mrs. Smith.

[2] Michael Taney was the ancestor of the late Chief Justice of the United States.

at Charlestown, because he would not acknowledge their authority.

Jacob Leisler, alarming the fanatical Protestants of New York Colony, about the same time, overturned that Government, and frequent correspondence was had with Coode.

Leisler, on the twenty-fifth of August, informed Governor Treat, of Connecticut, that one man had arrived in New York who affirmed that, "at the head of Patapsque," there were murdered, ten days before, whole families—one woman only escaping, and that it was found out by their habits that they were Canada Indians.

On the eighteenth of September, the Assembly of Maryland proposed mutual correspondence with that of New York. Capt. William Harris, one of the delegates, bore the letter, and the proposition was heartily embraced.

Coode, on the twenty-fifth of November, wrote to Leisler: "I believe our great men of this province, some of yours and New England, were a cabal, and held a correspondence against the Protestant interest, as it was, and is the endeavors of the Papist world; beside which observation we made betore our motion here, from several and frequent messages from your parts hither, especially to the priests, who have always been the chief sharers of the management of intrigues, against the Protestants.

"Three of our Popish governors are fled—

Darnall, Josephs,[1] and Sewall;[2] we have two only in custody—one Pye,[3] and Hill;[4] which three had a design toward your parts. They have with them a small yacht and brigantine; if they be not retaken—we have sent after them—we desire you will please to be as kind as circumstances will permit."

The excitement was increased at this time by Sewall's servants killing John Paine, who had succeeded Rousby, the King's collector, who had been murdered by Talbot. They were immediately seized, tried, and executed.

Kenelm Cheseldyn, Speaker of the Assembly, on April third, 1690, expresses "their sorrow at the massacre of Schenectady," and also informs Leisler, that they have voted speedy aid and assistance; and a few weeks later, Wm. Blanken-

---

[1] William Josephs was President of the Council. His associates were Henry Darnall, Nicholas Sewall, William Burgess, father-in-law of Sewall; Colonel Talbot, cousin of Baltimore; William Digges, John Darnall, Thomas Taillor, of the Ridge of Anne Arundel; Vincent Lowe, Surveyor-General; William Stevens, and Clement Hill, Deputy Commissioner.

[2] Near the mouth of the Patuxent, originally dwelt the Mattapanients, and here the Jesuits erected a storehouse, which was subsequently given to Henry Sewall by the Proprietary. His widow Jane, Charles Lord Baltimore married, and at this point, says Oldmixon, he built a house, "for convenience rather than magnificence." Nicholas Sewall, a step-son of Lord Baltimore, is the one alluded to by Coode.

[3] Probably Pyle, a prominent Roman Catholic of that day.

[4] Clement Hill.

stein and Amos Nicholls were appointed Agents for Maryland, to reside at New York.

King William expressed his approbation of the acts of the Protestant associators, and authorized the leaders to continue as officers *ad interim.* Lord Baltimore was also outlawed, but in 1691 the King reversed the decree, while he deprived him of the political administration of the province.

Lyonel Copley, on April ninth, 1692, appeared before the Assembly of Maryland, with a royal commission, and was immediately recognized as Governor.

One of the first steps taken, was to abolish the law protecting all classes of Christians, enacted in the days of the English civil war; and in an act entitled, "For the service of Almighty God, and the establishment of the Protestant religion," passed in 1692, and in another law of the year 1694, the Church of England was made the established church of the colony, and the privilege of public worship was not allowed to Roman Catholics. The Assembly of the year 1695 annulled the acts of the two previous years, and in 1696, it was enacted, that the Church of England in the colony, should enjoy all the rights established by law in the Kingdom of England, in all matters, not provided for by the laws of the province. The Quakers sent an agent to England, to prevent the approval of such partial legislation, and in 1699 the law was annulled by the order of the Council of Great Britain, and it was a bitter pill to swallow, for bigoted Church of England men in the colony, that a Quaker should have been appointed the bearer of the dispatch, conveying the intelligence.

Not only Quakers, but Roman Catholics, were beginning to be ostracised, as the following address of the Assembly of 1697 to the Governor will clearly show:

"Upon reading a certain letter from a reverend minister of the Church of England, complaining to your Excellency, how that the Popish priests in Charles County do of their own accord, in this violent and raging mortality in that County, make it their business to go up and down the country to persons' houses when dying, and *phranticke*, and endeavor to seduce and make proselytes of them, and in such condition boldly presume to administer the sacraments to them; we have put it to the vote in this house, if a law shall be made to restrain such, their presumption, and have concluded not to make such law at present, but humbly to entreat your Excellency, that you would be pleased to issue your proclamation, to restrain and prohibit such, their extravagant and presumptuous behavior."

In 1700, however, a law was passed "prohibiting the extravagant behavior" of all, but one sect, which met the approval of the King, requiring the Church of England to be the established church, and to be supported by general taxation. The law was totally opposed to the spirit that had prevailed in the colony relative to religion, and every fair-minded man in this tolerant age is sure to adopt the opinion of a minister of the Church of England, and a chaplain of Queen Victoria, who in analyzing it has said, "it contravened not only the statutes of William, but the toleration act of 1689; it violated the unalterable principles of justice."[1]

It was robbed of some of its harshest features, however, by its first operations having been superintended by a truly good man, the Rev. Dr. Thomas Bray, who, from a desire to see Christianity planted in the distant settlements of the New World, had at home established a Society for the Propagation of the Gospel in the Plantations. Visiting Annapolis, he passed the year 1700 in becoming acquainted with their spiritual destitutions, and returned to England to plead, with a facile pen and burning heart, for parochial libraries, and an earnest ministry for those of his emigrant countrymen who knew not God. By his influence mainly, Evan Evans,[2] Jacob

---

[1] Anderson, in Hist. of Colonial Churches.

[2] Evans was a Welshman, first settled in Philadelphia, at Christ Church, afterwards Rector of St. George's Parish, in Harford County. He died in 1721.

Henderson,[1] and others, became rectors and an honor to religion; while many emigrated, who were drones in the hive, and seemed more anxious to secure the pound of tobacco mentioned in the bond, than to win souls for a better world.

During the eighteenth century, there were several quiet, unobtrusive colleagues who did what they could to elevate mankind; Brogden,[2] Cradock,[3] Eversfield,[4] whose names are still pre-

---

[1] Jacob Henderson was born in Ireland; was settled in Dover, Del. In 1712 came to the Patuxent, and married the widow of Mareen Duval. He built what was called Henderson's Chapel. In 1716 was appointed, by the Bishop of London, Commissary on the Western Shore of Maryland. The next year he was Rector of Queen Anne's Parish, in Prince George's County. In 1729 the Bishop of London made him Commissary for the whole province. At times irascible, he was honest, godly, and useful, and died in 1751. Colonel Henderson, of the Marine Corps, and the wife of Gen. Lingan, were descendants.

[2] William Brogden was the son of a tobacco factor, who lived on the Patuxent, in Calvert County. He became a Deacon in 1735, and was ordained in England. Was Rector of All Hallows Parish, Ann Arundel County. In 1751 he succeeded Rev. Jacob Henderson, in Queen Anne's Parish, Prince George County. He died in 1770.

[3] Thomas Cradock came from England in 1742, and was Rector of St. Thomas's Parish, in Baltimore County. Dr. Allen, to whose sketches in Sprague I am indebted for a part of the material of these notes, says he was a fine scholar, and in 1753 published a version of the Psalms. He died in 1770.

[4] John Eversfield came from England in 1727. Rector of St. Paul's Parish, Prince George County. Near fourscore years of age; died in 1780.

A descendant, Charles Eversfield, is Surgeon in U. S. Navy.

served, and two, Bacon and Boucher, who were marked for superior mental ability, whose publications every Marylander, or son of a Marylander, will always peruse with interest.

Thomas Bacon was a native of the Isle of Man, and was educated by the celebrated Bishop Wilson, in whose diocese, his birthplace was situated. In the autumn of 1745 he came to Oxford, in Talbot County, and became the assistant of the Rev. Samuel Maynadier, who dying in a few months, Bacon was appointed his successor. After two years, he went to Dover, twelve miles distant, and there finding many poor negro slaves, as heathenish as when they or their parents were brought from the coast of Guinea, felt constrained to instruct them on the wayside, or in the houses of friends; and to exhort them at their funerals and marriages. Some of the sermons preached by him to the negroes, and also on the duty of Christian masters and mistresses, were printed in London,[1] and a few of them were republished in this country by the late Bishop Meade, of Virginia. He also, with the aid of contributions from Lord and Lady

---

[1] "Four Sermons, upon the great and indispensable duty of all Christian masters and mistresses to bring up their negro slaves in the knowledge and fear of God.

"Preached at the Parish Church of St. Peter, in Talbot County, in the Province of Maryland."

London: 1750. 142 pp., 18mo.

Baltimore, and their nephew his Private Secretary, erected in 1755 an industrial school about a mile from Oxford, the building for which yet exists. Bishop Wilson, a short time after, sent fifty pounds to aid in the instruction of negroes.

He next commenced a work greatly needed, a collection of all the laws of Maryland, as far as possible, from the time of the first Assembly. Before it was completed, he removed to Frederick, and from the day of its publication, in large folio form, it has been valuable to every lawyer, as well as to all those interested in the usages of old colony times. In this work he styles himself the Rector of All Saints' Parish, in Frederick County, and Domestic Chaplain in Maryland to the Right Honorable Frederick Lord Baltimore.

Jonathan Boucher[1] was not as practical nor as patient as Bacon, but for eloquent writing and extensive erudition he was the equal of any in the colonies. A sensitive gentleman, of strong convictions, a warm royalist, Rector of St. Anne's, Annapolis, and subsequently of Queen Anne's, in Prince George County, at the very time that the colonies were preparing to break loose from a government beyond the Atlantic, which was

---

[1] He was at one time the tutor of John Parke Custis, the son of Martha, the wife of George Washington, and his adopted child. In Sparks's Letters of Washington is a letter to Boucher, disapproving of the proposition relative to Custis making a foreign tour.

not adapted to, and could not be made to understand, their position and wants, it is not surprising that he should have sided with his friend Governor Eden, and looked with horror upon the rising spirit of republicanism.

Yet his very frankness and Christian fearlessness wins admiration, while the reader entirely dissents from the political theories broached in his sermons. His discourses on Absalom and Ahitophel were supposed to be aimed at Washington and Franklin. While he admired the former, he disliked the latter, and in a note to the discourse on Ahitophel he states: "It was in Philadelphia, if not solely, and by his friends, he was charged with having stolen from an Irish gentleman of the name of Kinnersley, many of his useful discoveries respecting electricity."[1]

Destitute of that fear of pewholders which locked the lips of some of the clergy, he plainly discussed all questions of the day, in their moral aspects.

In a sermon of the year 1763, he remarks:

---

[1] Kinnersley was Professor of Natural Philosophy in the College of Philadelphia, and brother-in-law of Edward Duffield, the life-long friend and executor of Franklin. The three were members of the American Philosophical Society, and frequently retired to Duffield's ancestral seat, near Philadelphia, to try experiments and make philosophical instruments. Kinnersley looked upon him as a co-laborer rather than a depredator of his scientific discoveries.

"Were an impartial and comprehensive observer of the state of society in these middle colonies asked, Whence it happens that Virginia and Maryland, which were the first planted, and which are superior to many colonies, and inferior to none in point of every natural advantage, are still so exceedingly behind most of the other British American provinces in all those improvements which bring credit and consequence to a country? He would answer: They are so because they are cultivated by slaves. I believe it is capable of demonstration, that except the money interest which every man has in the property of his slaves, it would be for every man's interest that there were no slaves, and for this plain reason, because the free labor of a free man who is regularly hired and paid for the work which he does, and what he does, is in the end cheaper than the extorted eye-service of a slave. Some loss and inconvenience would no doubt arise from the general abolition of slavery in the colonies, but were it done gradually, with judgment and good temper, I have never yet seen it satisfactorily proved that such injury would be either great or lasting."

A man who thus talked out his convictions, when "the times that tried man's soul" arrived, boldly took his position, which was in favor of the Crown, and ardent republicans soon made it too uncomfortable for him, to remain on this side of the Atlantic.

To a great throng he preached, in 1775, his farewell sermon, at lower Queen Anne's Parish, Prince George County. His text[1] was exceedingly significant, and concluding sentences full of pathos. "I confess to you there is something particularly ungrateful to my feelings in being thus outlawed and driven away from a country, where I have so long lived, with credit and comfort.[2] When I but little deserved it, I experienced patronage and protection. It was only when I came to render the best offices in my power to your country that I met with the worst returns. For these efforts to do good I have been attacked openly, and undermined secretly, ruined by the enemies of government without being either protected or pitied by its friends. In short, to borrow the words of a great man,[3] 'my life hath been threatened and my name libelled, which I count an honor.'"

---

[1] Neh., vi. 10, 11: "Afterward I came unto the house of Shemaiah, who was shut up; and he said, Let us meet together in the house of God, within the temple, and let us shut the doors of the temple; for they will come to slay thee; yea, in the night will they come to slay thee.

"And I said, Should such a man as I flee? and who is there that being as I am, would go into the temple to save his life?"

[2] He married Miss Addison, of Addison's Manor, which extended from the confines of Washington City to Oxon Creek. Oxon Hall is still standing, the old family mansion.

[3] Lord Bacon.

After he returned to England he became Vicar of Epsom, and devoted the latter years of his life in preparing a Glossary of Provincial and Archæological Words, which was published as a supplement to Johnson's Dictionary.

As one turns over the pages of Bacon's Laws of Maryland, he is astonished to find not a single provision for the education of the youth of the province during the first half century. Indeed, it is not until 1696, that any enactment is discovered. Then a law was passed for the establishment at Annapolis of a free school, to be called King William's School, "for the propagation of the Gospel, and the education of youth in good letters and manners." The corporation was made a body politic, by the name of the Rectors, Governors, Trustees, and Visitors of the Free Schools of Maryland, and were authorized to make rules not contrary to the laws of England and Maryland, nor opposed to the Canons and Constitution of the Church of England.

For the support of a master, usher, and scribe one hundred and twenty pounds were to be provided. After the school at Severn was established, it was enacted that there should be a second at Oxford, on the Eastern Shore.

But the law for years was of no benefit, as there were no funds. The Governor stipulated with Anthony Workman, that William Freeman, a bricklayer of Philadelphia, might build a house, to be employed by Workman as an inn, on condition that at his death, it should be for the use of the free school at Annapolis. Workman had a lease on life for several years, and ignorance increased, while the prospective temple of learning was a shrine of Bacchus, but at length the landlord rested from his labors, and the school reaped the benefit of the edifice.

In 1723 the school law was remodeled, and became the nucleus of those county academies in which so many of our ancestors were prepared for professional, mercantile, or agricultural life. The preamble of the Act to encourage education is in these words: "Whereas, the preceding Assemblies, for some years past, have had much at heart the absolute necessity they have lain under in regard both to duty and intention to make the best provision in their power for the liberal and pious education of the youth of the province, and improving their natural abilities and acuteness, which seems not to be inferior to any, so as to be fitted for the discharge of their duties and employments they may be called to, either in regard to Church or State."

The law then provides that the teachers shall be members of the Church of England, pious and exemplary in their lives, capable of teaching well the grammar, good writing, and the mathematics, "if such can conveniently be got."

Seven trustees were appointed in each county,

with power to fill vacancies, "from the principal and better sort of inhabitants." The first were named by the Assembly, and the roll of names, embodied in the law, is valuable, as showing who were considered the better and more intelligent sort of people at that early period.

SAINT MARY COUNTY.

Rev. Leigh Massey.
James Bowles, Esq.
Nicholas Lowe, Esq.[1]
Mr. Samuel Williamson.
Col. T. Trueman Greenfield.
Mr. Thomas Wanghop.
Capt. Justinian Jordan.

KENT COUNTY.

Rev. Richard Sewall.
Rev. A. Williamson.
James Harris, Esq.[2]
Col. Edward Scott.
Mr. Simon Wilmer.[3]
Mr. Gideon Pearce.
Mr. Lambert Wilmer.

ANN ARUNDEL COUNTY.

Rev. Joseph Colbatch.[4]
Col. Samuel Young.[5]

BALTIMORE COUNTY.

Rev. William Tibbs.
Col. John Dorsey.
Mr. John Israel.
Mr. William Hamilton.
Mr. Thomas Tolley.
Mr. John Stokes.
Mr. Thomas Sheredine.

CHARLES COUNTY.

Rev. William Maconchie.
Mr. Gustavus Brown.
Mr George Dent.
Capt. Joseph Harrison.
Mr. Robert Harrison.
Mr. Samuel Hanson.
Mr. Randall Morris.

TALBOT COUNTY.

Rev. Henry Nicholls.
Col. Mat. Tilghman Ward.[6]

---

[1] The Lowe family came into the province about 1675.

[2] Judge of Provincial Court.

[3] Ancestor of Rev. William H. Wilmer, D.D., and Bishop Wilmer.

[4] Ordained by Bishop of London. In 1694 became Rector of All Hallow's Parish. Died 1734.

[5] Judge of Provincial Court.

[6] Penn. Boundary Commissioner.

ANN ARUNDEL COUNTY.

Mr. William Lock.
Capt. Daniel Mariartee.
Mr. Christopher Hammond.
Mr. Richard Warfield.
John Beale, Esq.

CALVERT COUNTY.

Rev. Jonathan Cay.
John Ronsby, Esq.
Col. John Mackall.
Col. John Smith.
Mr. James Heigh.
Mr. Walter Smith, of Leonard's Creek.
Mr. Benjamin Mackall.

DORCHESTER COUNTY.

Rev. Thomas Howell.
Col. Roger Woolford.
Major Henry Ennels.
Capt. John Rider.
Capt. Henry Hooper.
Capt. John Hudson.
Mr. Gustavus Lockerman.

TALBOT COUNTY.

Robert Ungle, Esq.
Mr. Robert Goldsborough.[1]
Mr. William Clayton.
Mr. John Oldham.
Mr. Thomas Bozman.[2]

SOMERSET COUNTY.

Rev. Alexander Adams.[3]
Rev. James Robertson.
Mr. Joseph Gray.
Mr. Robert Martin.[4]
Mr. Robert King.[5]
Mr. Levin Gale.[6]

PRINCE GEORGE COUNTY.

Hon. Charles Calvert, Esq., Governor.
Rev. Jacob Henderson.[7]
Mr. Robert Tyler.[8]
Col. Joseph Belt.
Mr. Thomas Grant.
Mr. George Notley.
Col. John Bradford.

---

[1] Ancestor of the delegate to Continental Congress, and Governor and Robert Goldsborough, formerly U. S. S.

[2] Relation of the historian.

[3] In 1704 assumed the charge of Stepney Parish, and died in 1769, at the age of ninety-one years.

[4] Came from Scotland in 1706.

[5] Born at Lancaster, Pa., 1744.

[6] Major-General of militia.

[7] See page 181.

[8] Robert Tyler, the first emigrant, came to the province about 1660.

CECIL COUNTY.

Col. John Wood.
Major John Dowdall.
Col. Benjamin Pearce.[1]
Mr. Steptoe Knight.
Mr. Edward Jackson.
Mr. Richard Thompson.
Mr. Thomas Johnson, Jr.[2]

QUEEN ANNE COUNTY.

Rev. Christopher Wilkinson.[3]
Philemon Lloyd, Esq.[4]
Richard Tilghman, Esq.[5]
Mr. James Earle, Sr.
Mr. William Turbutt.
Mr. Augustine Thompson.[7]
Mr. Edward Wright.

WORCESTER COUNTY (CREATED IN 1742).

Rev. Patrick Glasgow.[8]
Col. John Scarborough.[9]
Capt. John Purnell.
Mr. Thomas Robins.[10]
Mr. William Lane.

---

[1] Ancestor of late U. S. Senator James A. Pearce.

[2] The first State Governor a descendant.

[3] Rector of Queen Anne's Parish, 1713. Died in 1729.

[4] Deputy Surveyor-General, and member of Pennsylvania Boundary Commission.

[5] Richard Tilghman, the emigrant, came in 1675. Had been one of the petitioners to have justice done to Charles the First. His son Richard married a Miss Lloyd. Represented by a late Chief Justice of Pennsylvania.

[6] Father-in-law of Tench Francis, Attorney-General of Pennsylvania.

[7] His father arrived about 1665, and married a daughter of Augustine Heerman, of Bohemia Manor.

[8] Had been a Presbyterian minister in Somerset County, but entered the Church of England, and became the first Rector of All Hallow's Parish, Snow Hill.

[9] Descendant of Edmund Scarburgh, Surveyor-General of Virginia.

[10] The ancestor of late Judge Robins, Rev. John Robins, and Thomas Robins, President of Philadelphia Bank.

WORCESTER COUNTY.

Major John Selby. Col. James Martin.[1]

These county schools were slowly organized, but after the war of the Revolution several became useful as academies, and that of Somerset at one period had a high reputation.

About the middle of the last century several brick churches were erected by law, a few of which are now kept in tolerable repair, while others are only frequented by bats and owls. There are two acts relative to the erection of a parish church in Snow Hill, one passed in 1746, authorizing a tax of eighty thousand pounds of tobacco to be levied, to be applied to church erection, and the other in 1756, granting the power to levy an additional tax of forty-five thousand pounds of the same article. In 1763 two hundred and seventy pounds of tobacco were equivalent to an English guinea, and at this valuation the whole tax was about four hundred and sixty guineas, which, like the tax for the support of ministers of Church of England, of forty pounds of tobacco for every taxable, was collected from all classes, without respect to their religious preferences.

[1] His son James, member of the Convention of 1788, for the ratification of the Constitution of the U. S. James Martin, a lawyer in Baltimore, and his sister, wife of Dr. John Neill, of Snow Hill, were grandchildren of Col. James Martin. Mrs. Judge Spence, of Cambridge, is a descendant.

In concluding a sketch of the established church of the colony, it will not be inappropriate to glance at the Presbyterian immigration. At an early period, some say as early as 1670, Colonel Ninian Beale came from Barbadoes[1] with a number of persons who were originally from Scotland, and occupied the region between Washington City and the Patuxent, a portion of which was called New Scotland. He is supposed to have been that "ancient and comely man, an elder among the Presbyterians," mentioned, in 1691, by the Quaker preacher, Wilson. He was intrepid and enterprising, and among the laws of 1699 is an "Act of gratitude" to Colonel Ninian Beale for his services upon all incursions and disturbances of the neighboring Indians, seventy-five pounds sterling, to be laid out for three serviceable negroes for him and his wife, and afterward for their children; the said negroes and their increase not to be subject to execution or judgment during his or wife's life.

Under the auspices of Colonel William Stevens, one of the councillors of the province, Somerset, then embracing Worcester, had received a large Scotch and Protestant Irish emigration, and he wrote, about the year 1680 to a Presbytery of

[1] Walter Bayne, of Charles County, whose place was called Barbadoes, one of whose daughters married Rev. Matthew Hill, and another John Beale, was probably of the same party.

Ireland, requesting ministers for that section of country. The first Presbyterian minister that arrived was Francis Makemie, who not only preached in the valley of the Pocomoke, but visited settlements in Virginia. His residence in 1690 appears to have been near the Pocomoke, in Accomac County, Virginia. The next year he was in England, where he probably published a catechism, which, in 1692, was read by George Keith,[1] the controversial and acrimonious Quaker, then visiting the Eastern Shore, who denounced the production as tending "to the Pope and Church of Rome." Makemie afterward published, at Boston, "An Answer to George Keith's Libel on a Catechism published by F. Makemie," which was recommended by Cotton Mather and other divines. At Edinburgh, in 1699, he published a book called "Everlasting Truths in a New Light." Another visit was made to England in 1704, and there a work from his pen was issued in handsome style, and dedicated to Edward Nott, Lieutenant-Governor of Virginia. It was called "A Plain and Loving Persuasion to the Inhabitants of Virginia and Maryland for promoting Towns and Cohabitation." Returning to the Eastern Shore, he assisted, in 1706, in organizing the first Presbytery in the United States, at Philadelphia, and was chosen its moderator.

---

[1] Keith was subsequently ordained by the Bishop of London.

Through his influence Hampton,[1] Henry,[2] and McNish came to Maryland. Lord Cornbury, Governor of New York, imprisoned him in 1707,[3]

---

[1] John Hampton was settled in Snow Hill in 1707.

[2] John Henry preached in Somerset, and married the daughter of Sir Robert King, and the widow of Colonel Francis Jenkins, who was President of the Council in 1710. He had two sons, Robert Jenkins Henry and John Henry, who became prominent citizens. John Henry, U. S. Senator from 1789 to 1797, was, I think, a grandson.

[3] The following letter, which seems to have escaped the attention of the historians of the Presbyterian Church of the United States, alludes to the formation of the first presbytery and his imprisonment:

Philadelphia, March 28, 1707.

MR. BENJ. COLMAN.

R'd Brother,—Since our imprisonment we have commenced a correspondence with our r'd brethren of the ministry at Boston, which we hope, according to our intention, has been communicated to you all, whose sympathizing concurrence I cannot doubt in our expensive struggle for asserting our liberty against the powerful invasion of L'd Cornbury, which is not yet over. I need not tell you of a pick'd jury; and the penal laws are invading our American sanctuary without the least regard to toleration, which should justly alarm us all.

I hope Mr. Campbell, to whom I direct this for the more safe conveyance, has shown or informed you what I wrote last. We are, so far, upon our return home; tho' I must return for a final trial, which will be very troublesome and expensive. And we only had liberty to attend a meeting of ministers we had formerly appointed here, and were only seven in number at first, but expect a growing number.

Our design is to meet yearly, and oftener if necessary, to consult the most proper measures for advancing religion, and propagating Christianity in our various stations, and to main-

because, while visiting that province, he preached without permission, and the proceedings at the trial are republished in the Force Historical Tracts. The sermon, for preaching which, he was arrested, was published at Boston, with this motto on the title-page: "Preces et lachrynæ sunt arma ecclesiæ." He died in 1708 in Accomac County, Virginia.

On the banks of the Patuxent and Potomac, at an early day, preached Nathaniel Taylor, Orme, Magill, and Conn. The latter was a graduate of Glasgow University, and came to Maryland in 1715, on the invitation of the merchants of Patapsco, and in 1719 moved to Garrison's Landing, as the neighborhood now known as Bladensburg was called. He died in 1752 while preaching at a funeral.

---

tain such a correspondence as may conduce to the improvement of our ministerial abilities, by prescribing texts to be preached on, by two of our number at every meeting, which performance is subjected to the censure of our brethren; our subject is Paul's epistle to the Hebrews. I and another began and performed our parts on vs. 1 and 2. The 3d is prescribed to Mr. Andrews and another. If my friends write, direct to Mr. John Yard, at Philadelphia, to be directed to me in Virginia. Pardon, sir, this diversion from

Your humble serv't, and brother in the
Work of the Gospel,
FRANCIS MAKEMIE.

Benjamin Colman, to whom the letter is addressed, was Pastor of Brattle Street Church, Boston.

On Bohemia Manor the Huguenots, and Reformed Dutch organized a Presbyterian church, and by the influence of Hutcheson, Professor of Moral Philosophy in the University of Glasgow, Alexander Hutcheson, of Scotland, in 1723, became pastor, and his elders were John Brevard and Dr. Peter Bouchelle, while the Bayards and Bassotts were parishioners.

In 1747 the eloquent and youthful Rogers,[1] the son-in-law of Colonel Peter Bayard, and the associate of Samuel Davies, preached with great success in Somerset, and William Winder,[2] a gentleman of culture, who had been a strong Church of England man, under his mild influence became a zealous Presbyterian, and did much to sustain the denomination in that county.

Among the first lay delegates to the presbyteries and synods of that church are found the names of Adam Spence,[3] Archibald Edmistone, and James Beale.

It was, however, a branch of the church not very well adapted to the condition of the province. To the luxurious and profligate it seemed

---

[1] Afterward pastor in New York City.

[2] Winder's daughter married a Mr. Morris, of Worcester County, and her sons were the late Dr. Morris, of Dover, Delaware, and John B. Morris, Esq., of Baltimore.

[3] Adam Spence was the ancestor of Dr. John S. Spence, U. S. Senator from 1837 to 1841, Judges Ara Spence and Thomas A. Spence.

austere, and to the emotional and illiterate its forms of worship were too cold. It has never yet been able to flourish, in a land destitute of school-houses, and where labor is not honored, having always felt that there was great significance in the old proverb, "Laborare, est orare."

CHAPTER SEVENTH.

SOCIETY IN EIGHTEENTH CENTURY, AND CAUSES WHICH LED TO INDEPENDENCE.

AT the commencement of the eighteenth century, the province contained many large land proprietors, and a few sparse settlements. Planters counted their acres by thousands, and a wilderness often intervened between them and their nearest neighbors. The country was so ribbed with rivers, that there was navigation to nearly every man's door, and it was with pride the planter beheld the vessel from Europe, sail up one of the numerous tributaries of the Potomac or Chesapeake, and unload on his own soil, the assorted cargo. The captains and crew of the colonial marine were well pleased with this condition of things, as their arrival, having been long looked for, and much talked of, they were always cordially welcomed; and during their stay, were not only the guests, but had the entire freedom of the neighborhood. A vignette on a map of Maryland and Virginia, published more than a century ago, represents a common plantation scene. A planter sits with easy dignity in front of his storehouse, smoking a pipe, and watching the slaves packing and coopering hogsheads of tobacco, intended for the return cargo of the ship, moored at the landing, while a half-nude negro is bearing to the captain of the vessel a waiter with glasses of wine.

With such facilities for shipping their products direct to Europe, they did not feel dependent upon commercial centres, and as there was no back country, there could be no large towns. Saint Mary contained about fifty houses, and Annapolis was not as large. A rhymer[1] of that era describes the latter as—

"A city situate on a plain,
Where scarce a house will keep out rain,
The buildings framed with cypress rare,
Resemble much our Southwark fair."

Slaves were rapidly increasing, and those directly from Guinea were but little above beasts of burden. It was necessary to commu-

[1] This extract, quoted by Ridgley, is from a satire entitled, "The Sot Weed Factor, or a Voyage to Maryland. A Satyr. In which is described the laws, government, courts, and constitution of the country; and also the buildings, feasts, frolics, entertainments, and drunken humours of that part of America. In burlesque verse. By Eben Cooke, Gent. Lond.: by B. Bragg. 1708." 4to. pp. 21.

nicate with them by signs; and to teach them the use of the plow, and other agricultural implements, was more tedious than the breaking of a horse to harness.

Others as dark as the native African, but born in America, were the principal field hands, and with an allowance of a peck of meal per week, and some salt, with such fish and game as they could catch, they were pushed by overseers to cultivate large fields of tobacco. Six thousand plants to the acre were usually planted, and each slave it was hoped, would make a thousand pounds. Bennett, the descendant of one of Cromwell's commissioners, owned thirteen hundred slaves, four hundred more than Col. Carter, of Virginia.[1]

Beside the negro slaves, there were indented white servants, or redemptioners, who served a stipulated period, in payment for their outfit and the expenses of the voyage from the "old country."[2] They were sometimes enticed aboard

---

[1] Douglass' Historical and Political Summary of the British Settlements in North America. London, 1749.

[2] In looking over some old family papers, in possession of a near relative, I find a letter from a Glasgow merchant, dated January 19, 1714, and addressed to "Mr. Thomas Mackey, merch't on Potomoak River."

After speaking of goods shipped, he writes: "The servants are all well cloathed, and provided with bedding, as ye will see."

He then states that some of the servants prefer "Mariland,

ships, by a class of men called "spirits," and brought to the colonies and sold.[1]

---

the reason whereof is that Virginia is a little odious to the people here." There were shipped on board the American Merchant, thirty-five women, thirty boys, and twenty-eight men. Subjoined are the names and occupations of some of the men and boys:

Names of Men.	*Occupation.*
William Colvin	Cooper.
Arch'd Williamson	Smith.
Peter Campbell	Coppersmith.
John Kennedy	Wright.
James Adamson	Sailor.
Daniel Millar	Shoemaker.
Henry Hunter	Tailor.
James Chrystie	Farmer.

Names of Boys.	*Occupation.*
Alex'r Campbell	Tailor.
Charles Swinton	Weaver.
Wm. Watson	Barber.
Peter Graham	Glover.
Henry McMillan	Butcher.
John Toward	Painter.
James Porteous	Baker.
Wm. Brown	Shoemaker.
Thos. Falconer	Farmer.

[1] Nearly two centuries ago, James Pancoast, a watchmaker's apprentice in London, was kidnapped and sold to a gentleman in Maryland. By his industry he obtained a tract of land at Gisborough, the point on the Potomac, in sight of Washington, used as a cavalry depot during the late war.

Having been drowned and unmarried, his estate was unclaimed for a long period, and reverted to the Proprietary. Two of his brothers, William and Joseph, were early settlers in

Later in the century, hundreds of paupers and convicts were also shipped from the cities of Great Britain, and such was the demand for labor, they were eagerly sought. A newspaper of the year 1737, under the caption of "An arrant cheat detected at Annapolis," states that a vessel arrived there, bringing sixty-six indentures signed by the Mayor of Dublin, and twenty-two wigs, of such a make that it was evident, that they were intended for no other use than to give a respectable appearance to the convicts, when they should go ashore.

Some of this class, removed from the corrupting influences of crowded cities, seemed to be able to overcome temptation, and made good and useful citizens.

At one period, the marriages between free-born English white women and negro slaves were so frequent, that the Assembly enacted that the wives of such should be slaves, during the lifetime of their husbands, and also that their children should be held in bondage.

In 1681, Eleanor Butler, or Irish Nell, as she is termed in the law reports, one of Lord Baltimore's domestics, was married to a negro slave, and her employer's influence was used to obtain

---

Mansfield, Burlington County, New Jersey, and years after the drowning of James, in 1770, the descendants of these brothers brought suit for the property, in the provincial court.

a modification of the law of 1663, but it did not prevent the enslaving of her offspring.

Planters often encouraged these alliances, from mercenary motives, so that it became necessary to make it a penal offence for any "master, mistress, or dame," to persuade or encourage a white woman to marry a negro slave.[1]

In 1719 the population of the province consisted of fifty-five thousand whites and twenty-five thousand slaves. Indolence on the part of the planters, and dependence upon irresponsible servants, produced the usual consequences, and the laws enacted during the first twenty-five years of this century, prove the prevalence of bankruptcy. To avoid their English creditors, planters, too proud to dig, fled from the plantations, while indented servants, by thrift and industry, soon became owners of the deserted estates. The "Gentleman's Magazine," of 1732, speaks of seventy planters of Maryland, in despair at the low price of tobacco, conspiring and destroying the plants of those who were still disposed to cultivate.

---

[1] The maternal grandmother of Benjamin Banneker, the mulatto mathematician and astronomer, who assisted Ellicott in laying out the City of Washington, was a white woman who married her negro slave.

Jefferson sent a copy of his almanac to Condorcet, Secretary of the French Academy of Science, who in reply wrote a complimentary letter to the Anglo-African. The Maryland Historical Society has published two sketches of his life. He was born in 1731, and died in 1804.

When the second Charles Lord Baltimore visited Maryland, the country had not yet recovered from the excessive cultivation of one staple, as the following lines, addressed to him, indicate:

"Too long, alas! Tobacco has engross'd
Our cares, and we mourn our markets lost;
The planters' crops, that overspread our plains,
Reward with poverty the toiling swains;
Their sinking staple chills the planters' hearts
Nor dare they venture on unpractic'd arts;
Despondent they impending ruin view,
Yet starving, must their old employ pursue.
If you benevolent, afford your aid,
Your faithful tenants shall enlarge their trade;
By you encourag'd, artists shall appear,
And gath'ring crowded towns, inhabit here;
Well pleas'd would they employ their gainful hands
To purchase and improve your vacant lands."

Toward the middle of the century, Annapolis began to be a centre of trade and fashion. Here the deputies of the Crown and Proprietary dwelt, and astonished the country people, by a poor imitation of the follies and vices of the English nobility, and introducing the French hair-dresser and dancing-master.

The style of the public buildings and private residences did not improve much before the Revolution.[1] The court house at the capital was

[1] Barnaby, an Archdeacon of the Church of England, who visited the place in 1760, says:

"Annapolis consists of about one hundred and fifty houses.

decayed, and "both without and within an emblem of public poverty," and a certain one of their own poets said:

> "Here, in Annapolis alone,
> God has the meanest house in town."

The other county seats were not superior. A writer in the *London Magazine* of 1746, describes Snow Hill as containing one brick house, the residence of the Church of England minister, and the frame houses as primitive in their appearance.

Living, as the large majority of the population did, on isolated plantations, hospitality was scarcely a virtue. The advent of a stranger was rare, and he was "sought after with greediness;" servants meeting him in the highways, by importunity compelled him to come to their master's house. Destitute of markets, provisions were abundant, and the tables were loaded with coarse but palatable food. At breakfast the guest was furnished with coffee or chocolate, hashed meat, venison pasty, punch, beer, or cider, and the dinner consisted of beef, veal, turkey, fish, and oysters. Having an abundance to

---

The town is not laid out regularly, but is tolerably well built, and has several good brick houses. None of the streets are paved, and the few public buildings here are not worth mentioning. The church is a very poor one, the stadt-house but indifferent, and the Governor's palace is not finished."

eat and drink, the population "became a careless, unthinking sort of folk."

As there were no commercial centres, ships came to plantations after passengers wishing to go to Europe.[1]

---

[1] By the kindness of a lady and former neighbor, a near relative of Lord Fairfax, I am permitted to publish a letter illustrative of the above remark, written by a brother of Governor Eden to Geo. Wm. Fairfax, who lived near Mount Vernon.

Annapolis, May 30th, 1773.

SIR:

I had the honor of receiving your letter of the 10th of May, sent us by Colonel Washington in his way to the northward. I had the pleasure of seeing him at Chester, on the Eastern Shore, but did not receive the letter, which had been (by my brother's desire, on account of the uncertainty of meeting me) left here for me, and I take the earliest opportunity since my return of answering it.

It will be agreeable to me to take agreeable passengers. The terms I have established are 20 guineas for cabbin and 10 guineas for steerage passengers from this country to London, and 25 and 12 from London to Maryland, on account of the estimated difference on the length of the voyage. As to passengers, I do not know of any except yourself and family whom I am likely to carry home this voyage, as taking passengers, unless to oblige particular friends, is not the plan I go upon.

Do not, however, imagine that I shall not be very happy in accommodating you and your family. With regard to provisions, you probably, sir, can be as good a judge as I am. You may, I think, venture to calculate the voyage for six weeks. Six hogs, and as many sheep, which latter ought to be accustomed to dry meat before they are put on board, with such geese, ducks, and fowls as you can (much more conveniently than I) put on board, will, with our own usual provisions and what I

In a country so new, the inns were mere stopping places to water the horses of travelers, and they were seldom called upon to lodge or entertain strangers. Gentlemen riding from Annapolis to Baltimore, in 1744, usually halted about midday at James Moore's, an ordinary house in a double sense, at the head of the Severn, and from thence drove to the Widow Hughes, at Patapsco Ferry, and crossing to Whetstone Point, proceeded to William Rogers's Inn, in Baltimore, which was three miles from the ferry.

When the Maryland Commissioners went to meet those of Pennsylvania and Virginia at Lancaster, for the purpose of holding a treaty with the Six Nations, the Hon. Philip Thomas, one

---

generally carry out of the country, suffice, unless you choose any one kind of provisions, and in that case you will lay in accordingly. As near as I can possibly guess, we shall sail by the last day of June, from Colonel Fitzhugh's, in the mouth of Patuxent River, where I should wish to receive you on board, and your sea stock, and should the ship be detained there a few days by any unfortunate delay, Mrs. Fairfax may be well entertained on shore by the worthy colonel and his lady, whom I reckon amongst my best friends. I should be glad to hear from you by the next post, as I shall not engage my cabbin, should it be applyed for, till I know your determination.

Please to direct to me under cover to the Governor here, who will know where to forward my letters to me.

I am, sir,
Your m't obed't humb. serv't,

THOS. EDEN.

of the Commissioners, Witham Marshe, the Secretary, and Rev. Mr. Cradock, the Chaplain, stopped at Moore's, and, says the Secretary, "such a dinner was prepared for us, as never was either seen or cooked in the Highlands of Scotland, or the Isles of Orkney. It consisted of six eggs, fried with six pieces of bacon, with some clammy pone, or Indian bread.

"But, as hunger knows little of cleanliness, and withal very impatient, we fell to and soon devoured the victuals. Our liquor was sorry rum, mixed with water and sugar, which bears the heathenish name of bumbo. Of this we drank about a pint, to keep down the nauseous eggs and bacon."

The night they were in Baltimore, the Rev. Mr. Bourdillon,[1] whose wife was a cousin of Lady Baltimore, paid them a visit.

On Wednesday, June twentieth, 1744, the party reached Nottingham, and here were joined by the other Commissioners, Edmund Jennings, Thomas Colvill, and Robert King, with the second Charles Lord Baltimore's natural son, Mr. Benedict Calvert.

---

[1] Marshe states that he came from England with Bourdillon, and landed in Maryland January 1, 1737. His wife was the niece of Sir Theodore Jansen. He became the Rector of St. Paul's Parish, Baltimore, in 1739. Previous to his visit to England, he preached in Somerset, and his first arrival in America was about 1735.

The next day the Commissioners and their friends arrived at Lancaster, Pa., then a town on the Indian frontier, and stopped at Peter Worrall's tavern. Marshe, in his journal, says: "Our Commissioners and company supped at Worrall's, and passed away an hour or two very agreeably; after which I retired to bed, but had not long reposed myself, when I was most fiercely attacked by the neighboring Dutch fleas and bugs which were ready to devour both me and the minister. However, after killing great quantities of my nimble enemies, I got about two hours' sleep. Mr. Calvert was more inhumanly used by them than myself, as was likewise Mr. Cradock. On the next night Mr. Calvert left our lodgings, and laid in the court-house chamber, among the young gentlemen from Virginia, who there had beds made on the floor for that purpose."

In honor of the Commissioners, James Hamilton, Esq., the proprietor of Lancaster, gave a ball, and opened it by dancing two minuets with two of the ladies here, "who danced wilder time than any of the Indians." Marshe adds: "The females—I dare not call them ladies, for that would be a profanation of the name—were in general very disagreeable. The dancers consisted of Germans and Scotch-Irish; but there were some Jewesses, who had not long since come from New York, that made a tolerable appearance, being well dressed and of an agreeable behavior."

After the treaty of 1763 with France, the grades of society became more numerous, and more distinct. The traveler found a few rich slaveholders, some enterprising farmers and merchants, and more listless, ignorant, indolent whites. "It is in this country," says the Marquis Chastellux, "that I saw for the first time, after I passed the sea, poor persons; for, in the midst of those rich plantations, where the negro alone is wretched, miserable huts are often to be met with, inhabited by whites, whose wan looks and ragged garments bespeak poverty."

There were in 1752[1] about three negro slaves for every white person, and a writer of that day says that the best-formed males were valued as "stallions" on an English estate.

Education was almost entirely neglected. The

---

[1] *Census of* 1752.

	Free.	Ind. Serv'ts.	Convicts.	Total.
Men	24,508	3576	1507	29,141
Women	23,521	1824	386	25,731
Boys	26,637	1049	67	27,752
Girls	24,141	422	21	24,584
Total	98,357	6870	1981	107,208

Whites	107,208
Negroes	42,764
Mulattoes	3,592
	153,564

wealthy were enabled to send their children abroad, but on their return, the young men, finding themselves surrounded only by inferiors, too often lost all interest in books, and became tyrannical or intemperate.

Boucher, in an address on "American Education," prepared for delivery at Port Tobacco, remarks: "At least two-thirds of the little education we receive is derived from instructors, that are either indented servants, or transported felons. Not a ship arrives, either with redemptioners or convicts, in which schoolmasters are not as regularly advertised for sale as weavers, tailors, or any other trade; with little other difference, that I can hear of, excepting perhaps that the former do not usually fetch so good a price as the latter. I blushed even for a heathen State, when I read long ago, in one of the most interesting moral writers of Greece, that they also were chargeable with an equally shameful and cruel instance of negligence. I do not mean to offend you, when I mention the sarcastic remark of Diogenes to the people of Megara. Seeing that they took great care of their property, and paid very little attention to the rising generation, he said it was better to be one of their swine, than one of their children."

A Presbyterian minister, settled at Upper Marlboro, advertised in 1722 for a runaway servant, who, from the description, must have been of the class of pedagogues to which Boucher alludes. The notice in the newspaper thus reads: "Ran away from the Rev. D. Magill, a servant, clothed with damask breeches and vest, black broadcloth coat, broadcloth cloak of copper color, lined and trimmed with black, and wearing black stockings."

Religion received as little attention as education. The majority of the freemen felt it was an imposition that they should be taxed to support a minister of the Church of England in whose services they felt no interest. While there were bright exceptions, many who officiated at the sacred desk, disgraced their calling, and the wags of the tavern supplemented the Catechism, by a significant question and answer:

Ques. Who is a monster of the first renown?
Ans. A lettered sot—a drunkard in a gown.

They were lineal successors of the fox-hunting parsons of Old England, and in a certain way accomplished, being competent, not only to unite parsons in the holy bonds of matrimony, but afterward to play the fiddle, while the company danced.[1] With a class of teachers and priests, "parasites and bottle companions of the rich,"[2]

---

[1] See Rev. Ethan Allen's Sketches in Sprague's Episcopal Clergy; also Bishop Meade's Old Parish Churches.

[2] Coke's Sermon in Baltimore, 1784, published in London, 1785.

it is not at all surprising that cock-fighting, horse-racing, gambling and intemperance, should have been common among parishioners.

Literature had few votaries. Some of the most active minds, were among the indented servants. The Æsop of the Province, George Alsop, at the age of twenty-eight, wrote a description of Maryland, which was published with a portrait and some verses at London in 1666, and he declared that he was happier as an indented servant in Maryland, than as an apprentice in that city.

Occasionally there may be found in the English scientific and literary journals, a contribution from some of the educated citizens of the colony. Mr. Richard Lewis published a poem in the Gentleman's Magazine, called "A Journey from Patapsco to Annapolis, April 4, 1730," filled with beautiful pictures of the opening spring. His descriptions of the mocking-bird, humming-bird, and an April thunder-shower, are equal to any in the American pastorals of the present century.[1]

While there was a lack of the education of the schools, there was, however, that strong feeling of independence always engendered in communities, which, by their own exertions, have subdued the wilderness and surrounded themselves with the necessaries of life.

---

[1] The poem in full is published in the Appendix.

In the eighteenth century, a large proportion of the freemen were natives of the province, and, as they had never witnessed the pomp of royalty, were not as much in awe of a King as their ancestors. Frequently the lower house of the Assembly intimated that the will of the people should be respected, and in 1722 they unanimously resolved "that whoever shall advance that his Majesty's subjects, by their endeavors and success, have forfeited any part of their English liberties, are ill-wishers to the country, and mistake its happy constitution."

From the time that every male, white and black, also black women above the age of sixteen and under sixty, were each obliged to give yearly forty pounds of tobacco to support ministers of the Church of England, there had been a growing coldness upon the part of many toward the British Government. The Roman Catholics particularly were dissatisfied. Not only were they forced to pay a church tax and twice as much land tax as Protestants, but were debarred the privilege of voting and of holding offices of trust and profit. The injustice toward them was so great, that at one time the father of Charles Carroll, of Carrollton, commenced negotiations with the King of France for a tract of land on the Arkansas River, where he might retire with his fellow-religionists. Immediately after the defeat of General Braddock, it was announced that several Roman Catholics had rejoiced that a priest had been seen on the frontier, in the dress of a French officer, and that they were in league with the negroes. The Rev. Mr. Chase,[1] Rector of St. Paul's Parish, in Baltimore County, declared that the situation of the Protestants of the province, was little different from those in Ireland on the eve of the massacre.

When, then, after the peace of 1763, the Stamp Act was passed, all of those in the colony opposed to arbitrary impositions of any description coalesced, and heartily united in support of the doctrine that there should be no taxation without representation.

The conservative Daniel Dulany, the leading lawyer, while not prepared to resort to arms, wrote one of the ablest pamphlets of the period on the impolicy of taxation, which was republished in England, and earned for him the reputation of being the Pitt of Maryland.[2] Those that were not held by official relations to the Proprietary,[3] the Crown, or the Church of Eng-

---

[1] Formerly of Somerset County, and father of the distinguished member of the Continental Congress, and colleague of Carroll.

[2] McMahon.

[3] The patronage of the Proprietary was very great. He had the appointment of—

land, generally adopted the view that it was the right of the colonists to be exempted from parliamentary taxation, and to regulate their internal government and polity. The delegates sent to the Continental Congress in every respect were representative men. The judicious Stone, the descendant of the early colonial Governor, the clear and logical Paca, the polished Carroll, the fiery Chase, were such as could not but exert a powerful influence in the deliberations of the body of which they were members. They were firm from the beginning, and repudiated half-way measures, convinced that there never would be a settlement of the point in dispute, except through the shedding of blood.

"We have completely written down our opponents," said one to Carroll, during the discussions previous to the assembling of the first Congress. "Do you think that writing will settle

---

Governor		Salary	£1550
Commissary-General		"	900
Secretary		"	800
Six Naval Officers	Each	"	150
Sheriffalty	"	"	200

In 1744 there was also in the Proprietor's gift—

Thirty-seven parishes	Each	120

If the clergy were once inducted no one could turn them out, no matter how scandalous their conduct, for there was no spiritual court, nor could any Bishop control, as the Proprietor was head of the Church.

the question?" asked Carroll. "To be sure, what else can we resort to?" was the response. "The bayonet," was the quick and decided answer. Chase having heard that the Rev. Dr. Zubly, of Georgia, a delegate, was wavering, rose one morning in Congress and in a speech of startling eloquence denounced him as a traitor, and the result was, that the suspected man never again took his seat.

The troops raised, caught the spirit of the eloquent advocates of liberty, and Smallwood's Brigade, in the early days of the conflict, earned a reputation for Maryland soldiery, which has always been sustained.

With the reconstruction of the State new religious and political forces were developed. On one of the little creeks that form the head-waters of the Monocacy, not far from the place where Bacon, the Rector of All Saints' Parish, Frederick, had laboriously completed a folio of more than one thousand pages of the Laws of Maryland, there lived a rough and honest backwoodsman, a recent emigrant from Ireland, named Robert Strawbridge. Filled with love for Christ, he began to preach in his primitive log-hut to the frontiersmen of the neighborhood, who knowing the purity of his life, and sincerity of purpose, heard him gladly. His circle of influence increasing, he at last entirely devoted himself to the work of the ministry, manifesting the noblest self-denial, and was the instrument of the conversion of the first native Methodist preacher in America, and also the founder of Methodism in Baltimore.

This form of religion seemed to be particularly adapted for the scattered settlements and worn-out parishes of Maryland.[1] The movement of the itinerants created as great an excitement as the preachers of the Society of Friends in the previous century, and the results of their efforts were more abiding. The work commenced by the pioneer of Sam's Creek was carried on by Asbury, who said: "The Lord is my witness, that if my whole body, yea, every hair of my head, will labor and suffer, they should be freely given up for God and souls."

A new impulse was given to Methodism in 1784 by a distinguished arrival from England. In the words of the *London Quarterly Review*, Asbury, "weary and worn by travel and preach-

---

[1] After the dissolution of church and state in Maryland, the Protestant Episcopal and Methodist Episcopal Churches, both outgrowths of the Church of England, commenced their career. The former succeeded to the forty or fifty parishes of the Colonial Church, and the prestige of a century; the latter was without influence, and with many uneducated ministers. The census of 1860 states that there was then in Maryland:

Protestant Episcopal Churches	158
Methodist Episcopal Churches	541

ing, arrived on Sunday, during public worship, at his friend Barratt's chapel. What is it that so strangely affects this self-contained and melancholy man, filling his eye with a strange light, causing the blood to crimson his pale and sombre face? There stands in the pulpit 'a man of small stature, ruddy complexion, brilliant eyes, long hair, feminine but musical voice, and gowned as an English clergyman.' With a beating heart, Asbury runs up the pulpit stairs, embraces him and kisses him before the whole congregation; for he is no other than Thomas Coke, LL.D., the man perhaps of smallest stature and largest heart that Methodism ever knew. He came direct from Wesley to cheer the heart of the lonely laborer, and to effect the most momentous revolution in American Methodism. He had been ordained 'Bishop' by Wesley just before his departure, and was in fact, despite all that high churchmen may object, the first Protestant bishop of the western hemisphere."

Many laymen, tired of the husks of religion, upheld those who seemed to diffuse its essence, and Richard Bassett, a descendant of the Huguenots, whose country seat was on Bohemia Manor, a member of the convention that framed the Constitution of the United States, Senator in Congress, and father-in-law of Bayard, one of the peace commissioners at Ghent, became a preacher of the Society, and like the Roman centurion, built a synagogue at his own expense.

Asbury and Coke, wherever they went, commanded respect, for they were not "mean men" in any sense. Though they exposed themselves to many hardships, and in the saddle rode over mountains and through forests, and preached in barns and the open air, to the bond as well as the free, yet they were not ignorant of the amenities of life.

Coke has left an interesting description of a visit to Washington, at Mount Vernon. "He received us very politely, and was very open to access. He is quite the plain country gentleman. After dinner we desired a private interview, and opened to him the grand business on which we came, presenting to him our petition for the emancipation of the negroes, and entreating his signature, if the eminence of his station did not render it inexpedient for him to sign any petition. He informed us that he was of our sentiments, and had signified his thoughts on the subject to most of the great men of the State; that he did not see it proper to sign the petition, but if the Assembly took it into consideration, would signify his sentiments to the Assembly by a letter. He asked us to spend the evening and lodge at his house, but our engagement at Annapolis, the following day, would not admit."

Not unmindful of the cause of learning, Coke and Asbury planned a college, and the latter laid its corner-stone in June, 1785, at Abingdon, twenty-five miles from Baltimore. It was called Cokesbury, a compound formed from the names of its projectors. The college edifice when completed was large and sightly, its curriculum extensive, including mathematics, Greek, Latin, and Hebrew, and at one period seventy students were enrolled. After an expenditure of more than forty thousand dollars, the library and building were entirely destroyed by fire, having had a brief existence of ten years.

The revolution in politics was as strange and sudden as that in religion. Successors were found to carry on the bold measures inaugurated during the war for Independence. Chase, attending the deliberations of a youth's debating society in Baltimore, was much impressed by the remarks of a "poor and friendless"[1] lad, who was a clerk in an apothecary store, and a student of medicine. He made his acquaintance, commended and encouraged him to study law in his office.

At the age of twenty-four, the now young lawyer, who had settled in Harford County, became a member of the Legislature, and in 1789, during

---

[1] Pinkney's description of himself, in a letter to Chase.

a debate on a bill regulating the manumission of slaves, delivered a speech which electrified his colleagues, and rendered the hitherto obscure name of William Pinkney familiar among the statesmen and philanthropists of America and Great Britain. His sentences were polished, and keen as the damascus blade. His voice was flexible and musical, but his eloquent denunciation of the system that had checked the prosperity of the land he loved, caused him to appear to the apologists of slavery like a destroying or avenging angel.

His words were as tongues of flame. A few only can be given in this brief sketch. "Iniquitous and most dishonorable is that dreary system of partial bondage, which her laws have hitherto supported with a solicitude worthy of a better cause. * * * * Eternal infamy awaits the abandoned miscreants, whose selfish souls could ever prompt them to rob unhappy Afric of her sons, and freight them hither by thousands, to poison the fair Eden of liberty with the rank weed of individual bondage!

"Nor is it more to the credit of our ancestors, that they did not command these savage spoilers to bear their hateful cargo to some other shore. * * * Never will your country be productive; never will its agriculture, its commerce, or its manufactures flourish, so long as they are dependent upon reluctant bondsmen for their progress. 'Even the very earth itself,' says Montesquieu, 'which teems profusion under the cultivating hand of the freeborn laborer, shrinks into barrenness from the contaminating sweat of a slave.'

"But it has been said, that nature has blackballed these wretches out of society. Gracious God! can it be supposed that thy Almighty Providence intended to proscribe these victims of fraud and power from the pale of society, because thou hast denied them the delicacy of an European complexion! * * * * But another objection occurs, which may deserve a more particular reply, because against that, there can be no adequate provision. Testators may impoverish their families, by inconsiderate manumission in their last sickness. They may be frightened by preachers, refined moralists, and others, when the mind is easily alarmed, and incapable of its moral resistance.

"I answer, that if emancipation can be effected with the owner's consent, while his understanding is legally competent to the act, I care not through what medium, fraud excepted. Should he reduce his family to beggary by it, I should not be the one to repine at the deed. I should glory in the cause of their distress, while I wished them a more honest patrimony."

These opinions, when read in the planters homes, startled the old régime into indignation; they appeared atrocious and revolutionary to those who had been trained to believe that the greatest slaveholder was the greatest gentleman of the land, and the name of William Pinkney was by such execrated; but the new element of society saw in him the brilliant orator, the sound statesman, the high-toned philanthropist, and they delighted in manifesting their esteem.

Although there had been an advance in society, after the close of the war of the Revolution, there was yet a deluded class continually sighing for the good old colony times, when commerce was restricted, political privileges few, ignorance rife, and religion in charge of hirelings.

The Golden Age many believed was in the era of the Baltimores, and that the reign of Maryland gentlemen had been succeeded by the rude sway of German, Scotch, and Irish traders on the shores of the Patapsco.

The revolution of 1689 developed new ideas and energies, which crystallized around Annapolis, and obscured Saint Mary, which from that time continually dwindled, and was only attractive to those who lived on the reputation of their ancestors, and clung to forms and theories simply because they were ancient.

The adoption of the Constitution of the United

States, in 1789, imparted fresh life to Maryland. Annapolis now became the seat of the old régime, while the City of Baltimore arose, the centre of new thoughts, and the depot of the produce of the western counties, rapidly developing under free labor. Hither the young, the energetic, the educated resorted, and white-winged commerce, in fleet clippers, bore its name to every clime.

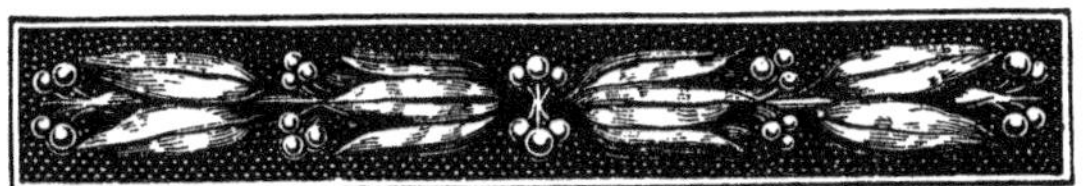

CHAPTER EIGHTH.

THE LORDS BALTIMORE AND PROPRIETARIES.

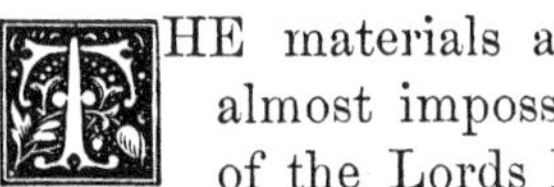HE materials are so meagre, that it is almost impossible to prepare a sketch of the Lords Baltimore and Proprietaries of Maryland.

GEORGE, FIRST LORD BALTIMORE,

was in talent, and in every respect, the head of the family. As early as 1603, was M. P. for Bossiney, in Cornwall; in 1621, for York; and in 1624, for Oxford University. In addition to the notices of his career in the first chapter, it may be mentioned that Samuel Calvert, a correspondent of one of the statesmen of that era, in a letter of April sixth, 1605, writes that "George Calvert hath good favor with his Lordship (Robert Cecil), and is diligent enough." In 1606 he was Prothonotary and Keeper of the Rolls in Connaught, Ireland. Winwood, as Ambassador to the States, had sent over to England a copy of Vorstius on the "Attributes of the Deity," with the remark that there was "matter enough in it for a wit that hath either spirit or courage." King James, believing himself such a wit, with the aid of Calvert, as has already been narrated, wrote a reply to the book.

A friend by the name of John More, writes to Winwood, on January first, 1611–12:

"According to your Lordship's command, it hath been my business to inform myself what construction is made of your late proceedings in the affair of Vorstius, which by general report I understand to have been exceedingly well liked by his Majesty, and Mr. George Calvert, falling of himself upon the subject at his house, whither I went with my wife, on a visit unto him and his, told me that the King had publicly declared that, in all the course of this business, Winwood hath done secundum cor meum."

On the eighteenth of February, 1622–3, King James granted to Sir George Calvert, in the County of Longford, Ireland, 2304 acres of arable and pasture land, and 1605 of bog and wood land, to be holden by knight's service. Two years later he was made Baron of Baltimore; and on March the eleventh, 1624–5, these lands were granted to him in fee simple, in free and common socage, as of the Castle of Dublin.

On May the twenty-ninth, 1625, King Charles writes to Lord Deputy Falkland:

"Right trusty and well-beloved cousin and counsellor, we greet you well: Whereas, our right trusty and well-beloved, the Lord Baltimore, hath acquainted us with his purpose to repair into that kingdom to reside there for some time; being an eminent person and a nobleman of that kingdom, we have thought good by these our gracious letters to recommend him to your special favor, requiring you not only to give him all lawful assistance and good expedition in such occasions as he shall have there, but also to respect him according to his quality and degree, and as one who is parted from us with our princely approbation and in our good grace."

On the eighth of August, 1622, his wife died. He survived until April fifteenth, 1632.

Children of George Lord Baltimore and Anne his Wife.

Cecilius, successor to the title.

Leonard, Keeper of the Rolls at Connaught from 1621 to 1626. Captain of a privateer off the coast of Newfoundland in 1629. Governor of Maryland in 1634, and died at Saint Mary on June ninth, 1647, without issue.

George, came to Maryland with Leonard, but is said to have settled in Virginia, where he probably died in 1667.

Francis, died in youth.

Henry.

Anna, married William Peasley, and lived in London.

Dorothy.
Elizabeth.
Grace, married Sir Robert Talbot, of Kildare, Ireland.
Helen.
John, died in youth.

Illegitimate Issue.

Philip Calvert, Governor of Maryland.

CECILIUS, SECOND LORD BALTIMORE,

before his father's death, was married to Anna, a daughter of Earl Arundel, who died at the age of thirty-four years, in 1649. Cecil was a member of Parliament in the year 1634. He did not possess the talent of his father, but was exceedingly politic. The following letter, written by him on May sixteenth, 1634, to Wentworth, Earl of Strafford, when Lord Deputy of Ireland, is preserved in the Strafford Dispatches:

"MY MOST HONORED LORD:

"Since my return hither to London, out of the country, which was about a week since, I had the honor to receive your Lordship's letter of the twentieth of April, wherein I perceive neither distance of place, nor greatness of employment, can any whit diminish that noble and true affection, which you have long professed, and many times very really testified to my father's family.

"Such an heroick virtue as that is, in your Lordship, can seek no recompense, but for itself, for it is much above all other means of requital; yet, my Lord, I will not omit the daily sacrifice of my endeavours to do your Lordship all faithful service, wherever I am, in perpetual hope of meeting some good occasion to testify my gratitude unto you, and that I may thereby in this particular confirm unto the world the greatness of your Lordship's judgment, as well as that other virtue of your goodness, in planting so much of your affection on me. I do most humbly thank your Lordship for your noble favours to my brother Talbot, and my sister his wife. They have let me understand that your Lordship hath amply performed, what you were pleased to promise me at St. Albans in their behalf. My Lord, I have many occasions from your Lordship to remember my dear Father, and now I do not want one, for I must confess I never knew any man have that way of doing favour unto others, with that advantage to themselves that your Lordship hath and he had."

Cecilius died on November thirtieth, 1675, and was succeeded by his son,

CHARLES, THIRD LORD BALTIMORE.

Charles became Governor of Maryland in 1661; married Jane, the widow of Hon. Henry Sewall, of Mattapany, on the Patuxent, and built "a fair house of brick," eight miles by land from Saint Mary.

After the death of his father, he visited England, but returned to Maryland, and while in the province had several interviews with William Penn. In 1684, he went back to England, and died on February twentieth, 1714, at the advanced age of eighty-four years. He was buried in St. Pancras' Church, Middlesex. He is said to have married three times.

The title and province became the possession of his son,

Benedict Leonard, Fourth Lord Baltimore.

Benedict Leonard was married on January second, 1698, to Lady Charlotte Fitzroy, daughter of the Earl of Litchfield, and grandchild of her whom Macaulay calls "the superb and voluptuous" Barbara Palmer, Duchess of Cleveland, and favorite mistress of Charles the Second. Until September, 1705, he lived with his wife, and had four sons and two daughters, but, following in the footsteps of her grandmother, a separation took place, and in 1710 he petitioned the House of Lords "to bastardize" her illegitimate issue. "Seduced by ambition and the efforts of the Queen of England," says McSherry, "and sustained against his father's opposition by a royal pension, he abandoned his faith to advance his fortunes." On January thirteenth, 1713, he publicly embraced the Protestant religion. Held the title of Lord Baltimore but little more than a year, and died on April sixteenth, 1715.

Children of Benedict Leonard Baltimore and his Wife Charlotte.

Charles, successor to the title.
Benedict Leonard, M. P. for Harwich, in Essex; Governor of Maryland, 1727. Died at sea, on his way to England, in 1732, and without issue.
Edward Henry; in 1728, Commissary-General and President of the Council of Maryland. Died without issue.
Cecil, died without issue, in 1765.
Charlotte, married Thomas Brerewood, Esq.
Jane.

CHARLES, FIFTH LORD BALTIMORE,

was born September twenty-ninth, 1699. He married on July twentieth, 1730, Mary, daughter of Sir Theodore Jansen. On January twenty-seventh, 1731, was appointed gentleman of the bed-chamber to Frederick, Prince of Wales; and on December the tenth a fellow of the Royal Society; was a man of culture, pleasing address, and elegant person, as the following poem in the Gentleman's Magazine of 1731, indicates:

"By heaven exalted, by your Prince caressed;
By nature favored, and by fortune blessed;
Complete in person, in address polite,
Fashion'd to please, to polish and delight,
Courteous to all, beneficent and good,
The best and purest marks of noblest blood,
True friend to science, and in taste refined;
To every study, every art inclined;
By all advantages of mind improved;
Admired, honored, courted, and beloved."

In 1732 he visited the Province of Maryland, and, returning in 1734, was elected a member of Parliament from St. Germain in Cornwall. From 1741 to 1747, he represented the County of Surrey, and died April twenty-third, 1751, aged fifty-two years. His wife survived until 1769.

Children of Charles Baltimore and Mary his Wife.

Frederick, successor to the title.

Louisa, married John Browning, Esq., and died at Horton Lodge, in 1821, at the great age of eighty-eight years.

Caroline, married Robert Eden, who was Governor of Maryland from 1769 until 1776, when he was obliged by the populace, to return to England. He returned after the war, soon died, and was buried under the pulpit of an Episcopal Church, on the north side of the Severn, two or three miles from Annapolis.

Illegitimate Issue.

Benjamin, called Benedict Calvert.

FREDERICK, THE LAST LORD BALTIMORE,

was born in 1731, and married Lady Diana Egerton, youngest daughter of Scroope, Duke of Bridgewater, who died in 1758, from injuries received by the upsetting of her carriage. He was sorely afflicted with "cacoethes scribendi," and in the Congressional Library is one of his books styled "A Tour to the East, in the years 1763 and 1764, with remarks on the City of Constantinople and the Turks. By F. Lord Baltimore. London, 1767."

The work is destitute of all pith. Walpole says "his bills on the road for post-horses would deserve as much to be printed. His book proves a well-known truth, that a man may travel without observation, and be an author without ideas." The Monthly Review of 1767 is still more severe in its criticism.

In 1768 he excited the indignation of the upright, and the ridicule of the rough portion of the London populace, by conspiring and forcibly abducting a beautiful and virtuous milliner girl. He was indicted for the offence, but acquitted; yet public opinion made it pleasant for him to leave the country.

No one can read the reports of the trial without having a hearty contempt for the man, and the following titles of a few of the poems, pasquinades, and exposures, issued within a period of a few months, evince the great excitement that prevailed:

"Memoirs of the Seraglio of the Bashaw of Maryland, by a discarded Sultana."

"Letter to Lord B——, with an Address to the town."

"The History of a late infamous adventure between a great man and fair citizen."

"The Rape, a poem, humbly inscribed to the ladies."

"Remarks on a pamphlet entitled an Apologist for Lord B——."

"Observations on a debate, made at a late evening's debate, at one of the Disputing Societies of this Metropolis, in their decision of the ravishing question, with suitable remarks."

"The Plain Question, Was she ravished or not?"

"No Rape, an Epistle from a Lord's favorite Mistress to Miss ——."

"A Letter on the behavior of the populace on a late occasion in the procedure against a noble Lord."

"The Trial of Frederick Calvert, Esq., Baron of Baltimore, in the Kingdom of Ireland, for a rape on the body of Sarah Woodson. Published by permission of the Judge."

"The Theory and Practice of Rapes, investigated and illustrated in an address to Lord Baltimore, and Miss Woodson."

Seeking retirement from his infamy, he published at Augsburg, in 1769, "Gaudia Poetica," a thin quarto of prose and poetry, dedicated to Linnæus, the botanist, which is celebrated not only for its insipidity but great rarity, always bringing a good price when exposed for sale. In 1771 he published another work, "Cœlestes et Inferi," at Venice. In the State Library of New York there is a copy of each.

At the age of forty, he died in Italy, in 1771, without lawful issue, and the title became extinct. He left his property to an illegitimate son, Henry Harford, Esq., a name perpetuated by a County of Maryland, with a reversion to Mrs. Windham, Mr. Harford's sister, who was first clandestinely married to Mr. Morris and divorced.

As George was the first, wisest, and best, so Frederick was the last, weakest, and worst of the

BARONS OF BALTIMORE.

Appendix.

A Journey from Patapsco in Maryland to Annapolis, April 4th, 1730.[1]

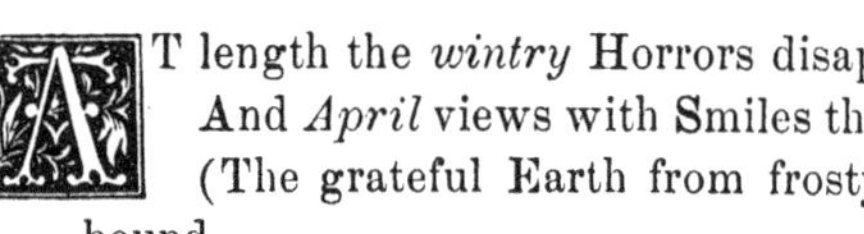

AT length the *wintry* Horrors disappear,
And *April* views with Smiles the infant year;
(The grateful Earth from frosty Chains unbound,
Pours out its *vernal* Treasures all around,
Her Face bedeckt with grass, with buds the Trees are crown'd,)
In this soft season, 'ere the Dawn of Day,
I mount my Horse, and lonely take my Way,
From woody Hills that shade Patapsko's Head,
(In whose deep Vales he makes his stony Bed,
From whence he rushes with resistless Force,
Tho' huge rough Rocks retard his rapid course,)

[1] The spelling, capital, and italicized letters are copied from the poem as it appears in volume second of the *Gentleman's Magazine*.

Down to *Annapolis*, on the smooth Stream
Which took from the fair *Anne-Arundel* its Name.
And now the *Star** that ushers in the Day,
"Begins to pale her ineffectual Ray.
The *Moon*, with blunted Horns, now shines less bright,
Her fading Face eclips'd with growing light;
The fleecy Clouds with streaky Lustre glow,
And Day quits Heav'n to view the Earth below.
O'er yon tall *Pines* the *Sun* shews half his Face,
And fires their floating Foliage with his Rays;
Now sheds aslant on Earth his lightsome Beams,
That trembling shine in many colour'd Streams;
Slow-rising from the Marsh, the Mist recedes,
The Trees, emerging, rear their dewy Heads;
Their dewy Heads the *Sun* with Pleasure views,
And brightens into Pearls the pendent Dews.
The *Beasts* uprising, quit their leafy Beds,
And to the cheerful *Sun* erect their Heads;
All joyful rise, except the filthy *Swine*,
On obscene Litter stretch'd they snore supine:
In vain the Day awakes, Sleep seals their Eyes,
Till Hunger breaks the Band and bids them rise.
Mean while the *Sun* with more exalted Ray,
From cloudless Skies distributes riper Day;
Thro' sylvan Scenes my Journey I pursue,
Ten thousand Beauties rising to my View;
Which kindle in my Breast poetic Flame,
And bid me my *Creator's* Praise proclaim;
Tho' my low Verse ill-suits the noble Theme.

---

* Venus.

Here various Flow'rets grace the teeming Plains,
Adorn'd by Nature's Hand with beauteous strains,
First-born of *Spring*, here the Pæone appears,
Whose golden Root a silver Blossom rears.
In spreading Tufts, see the *Crowfoot* blue,
On whose green Leaves still shines a globous Dew;
Behold the *Cinque-foil*, with its dazling Dye
Of flaming yellow, wounds the tender Eye:
But there, enclos'd the grassy *Wheat* is seen,
To heal the aching sight with cheerful Green.
Safe in yon Cottage dwells the *Monarch Swain*,
His *Subject Flocks*, close-grazing, hide the Plain;
For him they live; and die t' uphold his Reign.
Viands unbought his well-till'd Lands afford,
And smiling *Plenty* waits upon his Board;
Health shines with sprightly Beams around his Head,
And *Sleep*, with downy Wings o'er-shades his Bed,
His *Sons* robust his daily Labours share,
Patient of Toil, Companions of his care:
And all their Toils with sweet Success are crown'd.
In graceful Ranks there Trees adorn the Ground
The *Peach*, the *Plum*, the *Apple*, here are found;
Delicious Fruits! Which from their Kernels rise,
So fruitful is the Soil—so mild the Skies.
The lowly *Quince* yon sloping Hill o'er shades,
Here lofty *Cherry-Trees* erect their Heads;
High in the Air each spiry Summit waves,
Whose Blooms thick-springing yield no Space for Leaves;
Evolving Odours fill the ambient air,
The *Birds* delighted to the Grove repair:

On ev'ry Tree behold a tuneful Throng,
The vocal Vallies echo to their song.
But what is *He** who perch'd above the rest,
Pours out such various Musick from his Breast!
His Breast, whose Plumes a cheerful White display,
His quiv'ring Wings are dress'd in sober Grey.
Sure, all the *Muses*, this their Bird inspire!
And *He*, alone, is equal to the Choir
Of warbling Songsters who around him play,
While, Echo like, *He* answers ev'ry Lay.
The chirping *Lark* now sings with sprightly Note,
Responsive to her Strain *He* shapes his Throat,
Now the poor widow'd *Turtle* wails her mate,
While in soft Sounds *He* cooes to mourn his Fate.
Oh sweet Musician, thou dost far excel
The soothing Song of pleasing *Philomel!*
Sweet is her Song, but in few Notes confin'd;
But thine, thou *Mimic* of the feath'ry Kind,
Runs thro' all Notes! *Thou* only know'st them *All*,
At once the *Copy* and th' *Original*.
My *Ear* thus charm'd, my *Eye* with Pleasure sees
Hov'ring about the Flow'rs th' industrious *Bees*.
Like them in size, the *Humming-Bird* I view,
Like them, He *sucks* his Food, the Honey Dew,
With nimble Tongue, and Beak of Jetty Hue.
He takes with rapid Whirl his noisy Flight,
His gemmy Plumage strikes the Gazer's Sight,
And as he moves his ever-flutt'ring Wings,
Ten thousand Colours he around him flings.

---

* The Mock-Bird.

Now I behold the Em'rald's vivid Green,
Now scarlet, now a purple Die is seen;
In brightest Blue, his Breast He now arrays,
Then strait his Plumes emit a golden Blaze.
Thus whirring round he flies, and varying still,
He mocks the *Poet's* and the *Painter's* skill;
Who may for ever strive with fruitless Pains,
To catch and fix those beauteous changeful Stains;
While Scarlet now, and now the Purple shines,
And Gold to Blue its transient Gloss resigns.
Each quits, and quickly each resumes its Place,
And ever-varying Dies each other chase
Smallest of Birds, what Beauties shine in thee!
A living *Rainbow* on thy Breast I see.
Oh had that *Bard,** in whose heart-pleasing Lines,
The *Phœnix* in a Blaze of Glory shines,
Beheld those Wonders which are shewn in Thee,
That Bird had lost his Immortality!
Thou in His verse hadst stretch'd thy fluttering Wing
Above all other Birds, their beauteous King.
But now th' enclos'd Plantation I forsake,
And onwards thro' the Woods my Journey take;
The level Road, the longsome Way beguiles,
A blooming Wilderness around me smiles;
Here hard *Oak*, there fragrant *Hick'ry* grows,
Their bursting Buds the tender Leaves disclose;
The tender Leaves in downy Robes appear,
Trembling, they seem to move with cautious Fear,
Yet new to Life, and Strangers to the Air.

---

* Claudian.

Here stately *Pines* unite their whisp'ring Heads,
And with a solemn Gloom embrown the Glades.
See there a green *Savâna* opens wide,
Thro' which smooth Streams in wanton Mazes glide;
Thick-branching Shrubs o'erhang the silver Streams,
Which scarcely deign t' admit the solar Beams.
While with Delight on this soft Scene I gaze,
The *Cattle* upward look, and cease to graze,
But into covert run thro' various Ways.
And now the Clouds in black Assemblage rise,
And dreary Darkness overspreads the Skies,
Thro' which the Sun strives to transmit his Beams,
" But sheds his sickly Light in straggling Streams.
Hush'd is the Music of the wood-land Choir,
Fore-knowing of the Storm, the Birds retire
For Shelter, and forsake the shrubby Plains,
And a dumb Horror thro' the Forest reigns;
In that lone House which opens wide its Door,
Safe may I tarry till the Storm is o'er.
Hark how the *Thunder* rolls with solemn Sound!
And see the forceful Lightning dart a Wound
On yon tall Oak! Behold its Top laid bare!
Its Body rent, and scatter'd thro' the Air
The Splinters fly! Now—now the *Winds* arise,
From different Quarters of the low'ring Skies;
Forth-issuing fierce, the *West* and *South* engage,
The waving Forest bends beneath their Rage:
But where the winding Valley checks their course,
They roar and ravage with redoubled Force;
With circling Sweep in dreadful Whirlwinds move
And from its Roots tear up the gloomy Grove,

Down-rushing fall the Trees, and beat the Ground,
In Fragments flie the shatter'd Limbs around;
Tremble the Under-Woods, the Vales resound.
Follows, with patt'ring Noise, the icy *Hail*,
And *Rain*, fast falling floods the lowly Vale.
Again the *Thunders* roll, the *Lightnings* fly,
And as they first disturb'd, now clear the Sky;
For lo, the Gust decreases by Degrees,
The dying *Winds* but sob amidst the Trees;
With pleasing Softness falls the silver Rain,
Thro' which at first faint-gleaming o'er the Plain,
The Orb of Light scarce darts a watry Ray
To gild the Drops that fall from ev'ry Spray;
But soon the dusky Vapours are dispell'd,
And thro' the Mist that late his Face conceal'd,
Burst the broad *Sun* triumphant in a Blaze
Too keen for Sight—Yon Cloud refracts his Rays,
The mingling Beams compose th' *ethereal Bow*,
How sweet, how soft, its melting Colours glow!
Gaily they shine, by heav'nly Pencils laid,
Yet vanish swift, How soon does *Beauty* fade!
The *Storm* is past, my Journey I renew,
And a new Scene of Pleasure greets my view:
Wash'd by the copious Rain the gummy *Pine*,
Does cheerful, with unsully'd Verdure shine!
The *Dogwood* Flow'rs assume a snowy white,
The *Maple* blushing gratifies the Light:
No verdant Leaves the lovely *Red-Bud* grace,
Carnation Blossoms now supply their Place.
The *Sassafras* unfolds its fragrant Bloom,
The *Vine* affords an exquisite Perfume;

These grateful Scents wide wafting thro' the Air
The smelling Sense with balmy Odours cheer.
And now the *Birds*, sweet singing stretch their Throats,
And in one Choir unite their various Notes,
Nor yet unpleasing is the *Turtle's* Voice,
Tho' he complains while other Birds rejoice.
These vernal Joys, all restless Thoughts controul,
And gently-soothing calm the troubled Soul
While such Delights my senses entertain,
I scarce perceive that I left the *Plain;*
'Till now the Summit of a *Mount* I gain :
Low at whose sandy Base the *River* glides,
Slow-rolling near their Height his languid Tides ;
Shade above Shade, the Trees in Rising Ranks,
Cloath with eternal Green his steepy Banks :
The Flood, well pleas'd, reflects their verdant Gleam
From the smooth Mirror of his limpid Stream.
But see the *Hawk*, who with acute Survey,
Tow'ring in Air predestinates his Prey
Amid the Floods ! Down dropping from on high,
He strikes the *Fish*, and bears him thro' the Sky.
The Stream disturb'd, no longer shews the Scene
That lately Stain'd its silver Waves with green ;
In spreading Circles roll the troubled Floods,
And to the Shores bear off the pictur'd Woods.
Now looking round I view the out-stretch'd *Land*,
O'er which the Sight exerts a wide Command ;
The fertile Vallies, and the naked Hills,
The Cattle feeding near the chrystal Rills ;
The Lawns wide-op'ning to the sunny Ray,
And mazy thickets that exclude the Day.

A-while the Eye is pleas'd these Scenes to trace,
Then hurrying o'er the intermediate Space,
Far-distant Mountains drest in Blue appear,
And all their Woods are left in empty Air.
The *Sun* near setting now arrays his Head
In milder Beams, and lengthens ev'ry Shade.
The rising Clouds usurping on the Day
A bright Variety of Dies display;
About the wide Horizon swift they fly,
And chase a Change of Colours round the Sky:
And now I view but half the *flaming Sphere,*
Now one faint Glimmer shoots along the Air,
Now all his golden Glories disappear.
  Onwards the *Ev'ning* moves in Habit grey,
And for his Sister *Night* prepares the Way.
The plumy people seek their secret Nests,
To Rest repair the ruminating Beasts.
Now deep'ning Shades confess th' approach of Night,
Imperfect Images elude the Sight:
From earthly Objects I remove mine Eye,
And view with Look erect the vaulted Sky;
Where dimly shining now the Stars appear,
At first thin-scatt'ring thro' the misty Air;
Till Night confirm'd, her jetty Throne ascends,
On her the *Moon* in clouded State attends,
But soon unveil'd her lovely Face is seen;
And *Stars* unnumber'd wait around their Queen;
Rang'd by their *Maker's* Hand in just Array,
They march majestic thro' th' ethereal Way.
Are these bright Luminaries hung on high
Only to please with twinkling Rays our Eye?

Or may we rather count each *Star* a *Sun*,
Round which *full peopled Worlds* their courses run?
Orb above Orb harmoniously they steer
Their various Voyages thro' Seas of Air.
Snatch me some *Angel* to those high Abodes,
The Seats perhaps of *Saints* and *Demigods!*
Where such as bravely scorn'd the galling Yoke
Of *vulgar Error*, and her Fetters broke;
Where *Patriots*, who to fix the publick Good,
In Fields of Battle sacrific'd their Blood;
Where *pious Priests*, who Charity proclaim'd,
And *Poets* whom a *virtuous Muse* enflam'd,
Philosophers who strove to mend our Hearts,
And such as polished Life with *useful Arts*,
Obtain a Place; when by the Hand of Death
Touch'd, they retire from this poor Speck of Earth;
Their *Spirits* freed from bodily alloy
Perceive a Fore-taste of that endless Joy,
Which from Eternity hath been prepar'd,
To crown their Labours with a vast Reward.
While to these Orbs my wand'ring Thoughts aspire,
A falling *Meteor* shoots his lambent Fire;
Thrown from the heav'nly Space he seeks the Earth,
From whence he first deriv'd his humble Birth.
The *Mind* advis'd by this instructive Sight,
Descending sudden from th' aerial Height,
Obliges me to view a different Scene,
Of more Importance to myself, tho' mean.
These distant Objects I no more pursue,
But turning inward my reflective View,
My working Fancy helps me to survey
In the just Picture of this *April Day*.

My life o'erpast, a Course of thirty *Years*
Blest with few joys, perplex'd with num'rous Cares.
In the dim Twilight of our *Infancy*,
Scarce can the Eye surrounding Objects see.
Then thoughtless *Childhood* leads us pleas'd and gay,
In Life's fair Morning thro' a flow'ry Way :
The *Youth* in Schools inquisitive of Good,
Science pursues thro' *Learning's* mazy Wood ;
Whose lofty Trees, he, to his Grief perceives,
Are often bare of *Fruit*, and only fill'd with *Leaves ;*
Thro' lonely Wilds his tedious Journey lies,
At last a brighter Prospect cheers his Eyes ;
Now the gay Fields of *Poetry* he views,
And joyous listens to the *tuneful Muse ;*
Now *History* affords him vast Delight,
And opens lovely Landscapes to his Sight :
But ah ! too soon this Scene of Pleasure flies !
And o'er his Head tempestuous Troubles rise.
He hears the Thunders roll, he feels the Rains,
Before a friendly shelter he obtains ;
And thence beholds with Grief the furious Storm
The *noon-tide* Beauties of his *Life* deform ;
He views the *painted Bow* in distant Skies ;
Hence, in his Heart some Gleams of Comfort rise ;
He hopes the *Gust* has almost spent its Force,
And that he safely may pursue his Course.
Thus far *my Life* does with the *Day* agree,
Oh ! may its coming Stage from Storms be free,
While passing thro' the World's most private Way,
With Pleasure I my *Maker's* Works survey ;
With in my Heart let *Peace* a Dwelling find,
Let my *Goodwill* extend to all *Mankind :*

Freed from *Necessity*, and blest with *Health ;*
Give me *Content*, let others toil for *Wealth.*
In *busy* Scenes of Life let me exert
A *careful Hand*, and wear an *honest Heart;*
And suffer me my leisure Hours to spend,
With chosen *Books*, or a well-natur'd *Friend.*
Thus journeying on, as I advance in Age
May I look back with Pleasure on my Stage ;
And as the setting *Sun* withdrew his Light
To rise on other Worlds serene and bright,
Cheerful may I resign my vital Breath,
Nor anxious tremble at th' approach of *Death ;*
Which shall (I hope) but strip me of my *Clay*,
And to a better World my Soul convey.
 Thus musing, I my silent Moments spend,
Till to the *River's* Margin I descend,
From whence I may discern my *Journey's* End :
Annapolis adorns its further Shore,
To which the *Boat* attends to bear me o'er.
And now the moving *Boat* the Flood divides,
While the *Stars* "tremble on the floating Tides,"
Pleas'd with the Sight, again I raise mine Eye
To the bright Glories of the azure Sky ;
And while these Works of God's creative Hand,
The *Moon* and *Stars*, that move at his Command,
Obedient thro' their circling Course on high,
Employ my Sight, Struck with amaze I cry,
Almighty Lord! Whom Heav'n and Earth proclaim,
The Author of their universal Frame,
Wilt thou vouchsafe to view the *Son of Man*,
The *Creature*, who but *Yesterday* began,
Thro' animated Clay to draw his Breath,
To-morrow doom'd a Prey to ruthless Death ?

Tremendous God! May I not justly fear,
That I, unworthy Object of thy Care,
Into this World from thy bright Presence tost,
Am in th' Immensity of *Nature* lost!
And that my Notions of the *World above*,
Are but Creations of my own *Self-Love!*
To feed my coward Heart, afraid to Die,
With *fancied* Feasts of *Immortality!*
These thoughts, which thy amazing Works suggest,
Oh glorious *Father*, rack my troubled Breast.
Yet, *Gracious God*, reflecting that my Frame
From *Thee* deriv'd in animating Flame,
And that what e'er I am, however mean,
By thy Command I enter'd on this Scene
Of Life, thy wretched *Creature of a Day*,
Condemn'd to travel thro' a tiresome Way;
Upon whose Banks (perhaps to cheer my Toil)
I see thin Verdures rise, and *Daisies* smile:
Poor Comforts these, my Pains t' alleviate!
While on my Head tempestuous Troubles beat.
And must I, when I quit this earthly Scene,
Sink total into *Death*, and never rise again?
No sure,—These *Thoughts* which in my Bosom roll
Must issue from a *never dying Soul;*
These active *Thoughts* that penetrate the Sky,
Excursive into dark Futurity;
Which hope eternal Happiness to gain,
Could never be bestow'd on *Man* in vain.
To Thee, O Father, fill'd with fervent Zeal,
And sunk in humble Silence I appeal;
Take me, my *great Creator*, to *Thy Care*,
And gracious listen to my ardent Prayer!

Supreme of Beings, omnipresent Power!
My great Preserver from my natal Hour,
Fountain of Wisdom, boundless Deity,
Omniscient God, my Wants are known to *Thee*,
With Mercy look on mine Infirmity!
Whatever State thou shalt for me ordain,
Whether my Lot in Life be *Joy* or *Pain;*
Patient let me sustain thy wise Decree,
And learn to *know myself*, and *honour* thee.

INDEX.

22

ERRATA.

On page 133, Mrs. Burke *should read* Brooke.
" 166, more satisfactory *should read* not more.
" 190, Note 5, Born *should read* Commissioner.
" 191, foot-note number *six* refers to Wm. Turbutt
" 205, Barnaby *should read* Burnaby.
" 213, unite parsons *should read* unite persons.

www.ingramcontent.com/pod-product-compliance
Lightning Source LLC
LaVergne TN
LVHW010246110826
845151LV00004B/1404

* 9 7 8 1 4 2 5 5 2 3 2 0 6 *